HAWAII

POCKET TRAVEL GUIDE 2024

Explore History, Culture, Hidden Gems, Cuisine and Local Secrets in the Hawaiian Islands – Packed with Detailed Maps & Travel Itineraries

BY

MICHAEL VIANNEY

Copyright © 2024 Michael Vianney. All rights reserved. The entirety of this material, encompassing text, visuals, and other multimedia elements, is the intellectual property of Michael Vianney and is safeguarded by copyright legislation and global agreements. No segment of this content may be replicated, shared, or transmitted in any form or via any medium without explicit written authorization from Michael Vianney. Unauthorized utilization, replication, or dispersal of this content may result in legal repercussions, encompassing civil and criminal penalties. For queries regarding permissions or additional information, kindly contact the author via the provided contact details in the publication or on the author's official page.

TABLE OF CONTENTS

Chapter 1. Introduction.. 1
1.1 Welcome to Hawaii.. 5
1.1 My Experience in Hawaii.. 7
1.2 About This Guide.. 10
1.4 Travel Tips for Hawaii... 13

Chapter 2. Understanding Hawaii.. 15
2.1 Geography, Climate and Best Time to Visit................................. 15
2.2 History and Culture... 17
2.3 Language, Communication & Essential Hawaiian Phrases............ 18
11.2 Cultural Do's and Don'ts.. 20
11.3 Tips for Interacting with Locals... 21

Chapter 3. Planning Your Trip.. 23
3.2 Visa and Entry Requirements... 23
3.3 Health and Safety Tips.. 25
3.4 Packing Essentials.. 27
2.4 Currency Exchange and Budgeting for Your Trip........................ 28
2.5 Accommodation Options... 30
2.6 Getting to Hawaii.. 35
2.7 Transportation Options... 37

Chapter 4. Exploring Oahu... 41
4.1 Overview of Oahu... 41
4.2 Must-See Attractions.. 44
- 4.2.1 Waikiki Beach... 46
- 4.2.2 Pearl Harbor... 47
- 4.2.3 Diamond Head Crater.. 49
- 4.2.4 Polynesian Cultural Center... 50
4.3 Hidden Gems of Oahu... 51
4.4 Exploring Oahu's Neighborhoods... 54
4.5 Dining and Nightlife in Oahu.. 58
Chapter 5. Discovering Maui... 60

5.1 Overview of Maui.. 63
5.2 Must-See Attractions... 65
- 5.2.1 Road to Hana... 67
- 5.2.2 Haleakalā National Park.. 69
- 5.2.3 Lahaina Historic District... 70
- 5.2.4 Molokini Crater... 71
5.3 Hidden Gems of Maui... 71
5.4 Exploring Maui's Towns... 73
5.5 Dining and Nightlife in Maui.. 75

Chapter 6. Exploring Big Island (Hawaii Island)..................................... 77
6.1 Overview of Big Island... 77
6.2 Must-See Attractions... 79
- 6.2.1 Hawaii Volcanoes National Park.. 80
- 6.2.2 Mauna Kea Observatory.. 81
- 6.2.3 Hilo and Rainbow Falls... 81
- 6.2.4 Pu'uhonua o Hōnaunau National Historical Park......................... 82
6.3 Hidden Gems of Big Island.. 85
6.4 Exploring Big Island's Regions.. 87
6.5 Dining and Nightlife on Big Island... 89

Chapter 7. Discovering Kauai... 92
7.1 Overview of Kauai.. 92
7.2 Must-See Attractions... 94
- 7.2.1 Na Pali Coast... 95
- 7.2.2 Waimea Canyon State Park... 96
- 7.2.3 Poipu Beach Park... 96
- 7.2.4 Wailua Falls... 97
7.3 Hidden Gems of Kauai.. 97
7.4 Exploring Kauai's Regions... 99
7.5 Dining and Nightlife in Kauai... 102

Chapter 8. Immersing in Hawaiian Culture.. 106
8.1 Festivals and Events.. 106
8.2 Hawaiian Cultural Traditions.. 109
8.3 Arts and Music Scene.. 111

8.4 Luau and Traditional Hawaiian Cuisine.. 114

Chapter 9. Outdoor Adventures...117
9.1 Hiking Trails and Nature Walks... 117
9.2 Snorkeling and Scuba Diving Spots... 119
9.3 Surfing and Water Sports... 122
9.4 Ziplining and Eco-Tours...125

Chapter 10. Traveling with Special Interests................................... 128
10.1 Family-Friendly Activities.. 128
10.2 LGBTQ+ Travel in Hawaii... 131

Chapter 11 Practical Information and Travel Resources.................. 135
11.1 Maps of Hawaii; Oahu, Maui, Big Island and Kauai................ 135
11.2 Five Days Itinerary... 141
11.3 Safety Tips and Emergency Contacts....................................... 144
11.4 Shopping and Souvenirs... 146
11.5 Useful Websites, Mobile Apps and Online Resources............. 151
11.6 Internet Access and Connectivity... 153
11.7 Visitor Centers and Tourist Assistance.................................... 155
Conclusion and Recommendations.. 158

CHAPTER 1
INTRODUCTION

1.1 Welcome to Hawaii

Hawaii, a land of unparalleled beauty, rich culture, and unforgettable experiences that beckon travelers from all corners of the globe. Let's embark on a journey through this tropical paradise and explore what makes Hawaii a destination unlike any other.

The Aloha Spirit

When you arrive in Hawaii, you're not just visiting a place; you're immersing yourself in a way of life that is deeply rooted in the concept of Aloha. More than just a greeting, Aloha is a philosophy that embodies love, peace, and compassion. From the warm smiles of the locals to the harmonious blend of cultures, the Aloha spirit is palpable and infectious. It invites you to slow down, embrace the present moment, and connect with the people and the natural beauty that surrounds you.

The Islands' Diverse Landscapes

Hawaii's islands are a tapestry of diverse landscapes, each offering its own unique allure. Picture yourself wandering through the dense rainforests of Kauai, where waterfalls cascade down towering cliffs and vibrant flowers paint the landscape in a kaleidoscope of colors. Imagine standing on the volcanic sands of the Big Island, where you can witness the raw power of nature as molten lava meets the sea, creating new land before your very eyes. Visualize the serene beaches of Maui, where crystal-clear waters invite you to dive in and explore the vibrant coral reefs teeming with marine life.

Hawaii's Rich History and Culture

Hawaii's history is as rich and diverse as its landscapes. From ancient Polynesian voyagers who first settled the islands to the influential reign of King Kamehameha, the stories of Hawaii's past are woven into the fabric of its present. Visiting historical sites like the Iolani Palace in Oahu or the sacred Puʻuhonua o Hōnaunau National Historical Park on the Big Island allows you to step back in time and appreciate the cultural heritage that has shaped Hawaii into what it is today. Engaging in traditional hula dancing or attending a luau gives you a glimpse into the customs and traditions that continue to thrive in modern Hawaiian life.

Outdoor Activities and Thrills

For those with a thirst for adventure, Hawaii offers an abundance of activities that cater to all interests and skill levels. Imagine hiking the challenging trails of Haleakalā National Park in Maui, where you can witness a breathtaking sunrise from the summit of a dormant volcano. Picture yourself surfing the iconic waves of Waikiki Beach, feeling the rush of adrenaline as you ride the same swells that have captivated surfers for generations. For the more daring, the underwater wonders of Molokini Crater invite you to snorkel or dive in a submerged volcanic caldera, surrounded by vibrant marine life and stunning coral formations.

Culinary Delights

Hawaii's culinary scene is a delightful fusion of flavors, reflecting its multicultural heritage. Envision savoring fresh poke bowls, where the delicate taste of raw fish is perfectly complemented by a medley of seasonings and toppings. Indulge in the sweet and savory flavors of traditional Hawaiian dishes like kalua pig, cooked to perfection in an underground imu oven. And let's not forget the tropical fruits – juicy pineapples, creamy coconuts, and succulent mangoes that burst with flavor and freshness. Dining in Hawaii is not just about satisfying your hunger; it's about experiencing the vibrant culinary traditions that make the islands a gastronomic paradise.

Serenity and Relaxation

Amidst the adventures and activities, Hawaii also offers countless opportunities for relaxation and rejuvenation. Picture yourself lounging on the soft sands of Lanikai Beach, where the gentle sound of the waves lulls you into a state of tranquility. Envision a spa retreat where traditional Hawaiian healing practices, such as lomilomi massage, soothe your body and soul. Whether you're practicing yoga on the beach or simply enjoying a sunset with a refreshing mai tai in hand, Hawaii provides the perfect backdrop for finding your inner peace and recharging your spirit.

1.2 My Experience in Hawaii

The moment I landed in Honolulu, I was enveloped by the warmth of the Hawaiian spirit. The "Aloha" greeting from the locals felt more than just a word; it was an embrace, a welcoming into their world. My journey began on Oahu, the bustling heart of Hawaii. Despite its urban pulse, Oahu is a paradise where natural beauty and culture coexist harmoniously. The iconic Waikiki Beach was my first stop. As I sank my feet into its golden sands and gazed at the surfers riding the waves against the backdrop of Diamond Head, I felt a sense of serenity. The sunset here is a spectacle; the sky transforms into a canvas of oranges, pinks, and purples, reflecting off the Pacific. I spent hours walking along the shoreline, listening to the rhythmic crashing of waves, and feeling the cool breeze that carried a hint of salt and adventure.

However, Oahu's charm isn't confined to its beaches. Venturing inland, I hiked up to the Nu'uanu Pali Lookout. The panoramic view of lush green cliffs cascading into the azure ocean was breathtaking. The hike itself was a journey through history; this very pass was the site of a crucial battle that united the Hawaiian Islands. Standing at the lookout, with the wind whipping through my hair, I felt a profound connection to the land and its storied past. Leaving Oahu, I hopped over to Maui, the "Valley Isle." Maui is a contrast of rugged landscapes and luxury resorts. The Road to Hana, a winding drive through dense rainforests, past cascading waterfalls, and along dramatic coastal cliffs, was an adventure in itself. Every turn revealed a new marvel: the vibrant hues of Hana's tropical flora, the hidden beaches with black volcanic sand, and the refreshing plunge pools that invited me to take a dip.

In Hana, I stayed in a quaint cottage, where the absence of modern distractions allowed me to immerse myself in the natural world. One early morning, I witnessed the sunrise from Haleakalā, the "House of the Sun." Ascending the dormant volcano in the pre-dawn darkness, the cold was biting. But as the first light broke over the horizon, bathing the crater in a golden glow, it felt like a rebirth. The vast, otherworldly landscape stretched out beneath me, and for a moment, I was utterly at peace. The Big Island, Hawaii itself, offered a completely different experience. Here, I encountered the raw power of nature. At Hawai'i Volcanoes National Park, I stood in awe before the bubbling lava lake of Kilauea. The ground beneath my feet was warm, and the air was thick with the scent of sulfur. It was humbling to witness the earth's primal forces at work, reshaping the land before my eyes.

Equally captivating was the Big Island's Kona coast, where I snorkeled in the clear, warm waters of Kealakekua Bay. Swimming alongside vibrant coral reefs teeming with marine life was like entering another world. The playful dolphins that occasionally surfaced added a magical touch to the experience. Kauai, the "Garden Isle," was my final destination. Its untouched beauty is unparalleled. The Na Pali Coast, with its towering sea cliffs and emerald valleys, is best appreciated from the sea. I joined a boat tour, and as we sailed along the rugged coastline, dolphins danced in our wake, and sea turtles bobbed in the surf. The views were postcard-perfect, but being there, feeling the spray of the ocean and the warmth of the sun, was indescribably more powerful.

Hiking the Kalalau Trail was a challenging yet rewarding endeavor. The trail carved through dense jungle, crossed streams, and offered heart-stopping views of the coastline. Camping overnight at Kalalau Beach, I was enveloped by the tranquility that only such a remote paradise can offer. The starry sky above, untainted by city lights, was a mesmerizing tapestry. Throughout my travels in Hawaii, I was continuously moved by the deep sense of respect the Hawaiian people have for their land and culture. Their traditions, music, and dance tell stories of their ancestors and their deep connection to the earth. Attending a traditional luau, with its feast of kalua pig, poi, and fresh island fruits, was not just a meal but a cultural celebration.

Hawaii is a place that captivates the soul. Its natural beauty is awe-inspiring, but it is the spirit of Aloha, the genuine warmth and hospitality of its people, that leaves an indelible mark on the heart. As I left Hawaii, I knew that I carried a piece of it with me, a cherished memory that would forever fuel my wanderlust.

For anyone seeking a destination that offers more than just scenic vistas, Hawaii awaits with open arms and a promise of adventure and serenity intertwined.

1.3 About This Guide

Hawaii, with its lush landscapes, stunning beaches, and rich cultural heritage, beckons travelers from across the globe to experience its wonders. Whether you're seeking adventure, relaxation, or a taste of island life, Hawaii offers an abundance of experiences to suit every traveler's desires. Welcome to the Hawaii Comprehensive Guide, your passport to navigating this enchanting archipelago.

Maps and Navigation

Hawaii consists of six main islands, each with its own distinct character and allure. The largest and most populous is the island of Oahu, home to the state capital, Honolulu, and the iconic Waikiki Beach. Maui boasts stunning landscapes, including the lush Hana Highway and the otherworldly Haleakalā National Park. The Big Island, or Hawaii Island, is renowned for its volcanic wonders, including the active Kilauea volcano and Mauna Kea, the tallest mountain in the world when measured from its base on the ocean floor. To navigate these islands efficiently, consider downloading maps and navigation apps like Google Maps or Waze, which provide real-time traffic updates and directions. Additionally, many car rental companies offer GPS navigation systems as part of their services, making it easier to explore Hawaii's scenic highways and hidden gems.

Accommodation Options

From luxury resorts to cozy bed and breakfasts, Hawaii offers a diverse array of accommodation options to suit every budget and preference. Beachfront villas, eco-friendly retreats, and boutique hotels dot the islands, providing travelers with a range of choices for their stay. For those seeking a more immersive experience, vacation rentals and homestays offer the opportunity to live like a local and soak in the aloha spirit.

Transportation

While renting a car is the most convenient way to explore Hawaii's islands, public transportation, rideshare services, and organized tours are also available. Many visitors opt to rent a car to have the freedom to explore at their own pace, but for those who prefer not to drive, shuttle services and guided excursions offer hassle-free alternatives.

Top Attractions

From the iconic beaches of Waikiki to the volcanic landscapes of Hawaii Volcanoes National Park, Hawaii is home to an array of must-see attractions. Snorkel with vibrant marine life at Hanauma Bay, hike to the summit of Diamond Head Crater for panoramic views of Honolulu, or marvel at the cascading waterfalls of Maui's Road to Hana. Each island boasts its own unique wonders waiting to be discovered.

Practical Information and Travel Resources

Before embarking on your Hawaiian adventure, it's essential to familiarize yourself with practical information such as local customs, weather patterns, and safety tips. Hawaii's diverse climate ranges from tropical rainforests to arid deserts, so packing accordingly is crucial.

Culinary Delights

Hawaii's culinary scene is a melting pot of flavors influenced by its diverse cultural heritage. Indulge in traditional Hawaiian dishes such as poi, kalua pig, and laulau, or savor the fusion cuisine found in local food trucks and upscale restaurants. Don't miss out on trying shave ice, a beloved Hawaiian treat, or sampling fresh poke from one of the island's many seafood markets.

Culture and Heritage

Immerse yourself in the rich cultural heritage of Hawaii through traditional hula performances, lei-making workshops, and visits to historic sites such as Pearl Harbor and Iolani Palace. Learn about the significance of aloha spirit, ohana (family), and kapu (taboos) in Hawaiian culture, and participate in cultural activities to gain a deeper appreciation for the islands' history and traditions.

Outdoor Activities and Adventures

With its stunning natural beauty, Hawaii is a paradise for outdoor enthusiasts. Embark on thrilling adventures such as zip-lining through the rainforest, hiking to hidden waterfalls, or snorkeling alongside sea turtles in crystal-clear waters. For adrenaline junkies, surfing the legendary waves of the North Shore or embarking on a helicopter tour of the islands offer unforgettable experiences.

Shopping

From local crafts and souvenirs to designer boutiques and luxury malls, Hawaii offers a diverse shopping scene sure to satisfy every shopper's desires. Browse open-air markets for unique handmade goods, pick up traditional Hawaiian apparel and accessories, or splurge on high-end fashion brands in Honolulu's bustling shopping districts.

Day Trips and Excursions

Explore beyond the shores of your home base with a variety of day trips and excursions available throughout the islands. Visit the majestic Na Pali Coast of Kauai, embark on a scenic drive along the Hana Highway in Maui, or take a boat tour to explore the marine life of Molokini Crater. With so much to see and do, each day brings new opportunities for adventure and discovery.

Entertainment and Nightlife

As the sun sets over the Pacific, Hawaii comes alive with vibrant entertainment and nightlife options. Enjoy live music and traditional hula performances at luaus and dinner shows, sip tropical cocktails at beachfront bars, or dance the night away at clubs and lounges. Whether you're seeking a laid-back evening or an energetic night on the town, Hawaii's nightlife scene has something for everyone.

1.4 Travel Tips for Hawaii

From the instant you set foot on Hawaiian soil, you'll be enveloped in the spirit of Aloha—an ethos steeped in love, harmony, and kindness. Embrace this ethos fully, for it is the heartbeat of these islands. Take time to connect with the locals, absorb their stories, and dive deep into the cultural richness of Hawaii.

Delight in Island Flavors

Hawaii tantalizes not only with its stunning vistas but also with its delectable cuisine. Embark on a culinary odyssey, sampling the diverse flavors that make Hawaiian food so irresistible. From succulent seafood to luscious tropical fruits, each bite offers a tantalizing glimpse into the island's culinary heritage. Don't miss the chance to savor iconic dishes like poke, kalua pig, and shave ice—each a tribute to Hawaii's gastronomic diversity.

Explore Natural Marvels

The allure of Hawaii lies in its awe-inspiring natural beauty. From towering volcanoes to pristine beaches and verdant rainforests, the islands beckon adventurers and nature enthusiasts alike. Embark on unforgettable escapades—hike to Mauna Kea's summit for a stellar spectacle, snorkel in azure waters teeming with marine life, or simply bask in the sun's golden embrace on a secluded shore.

Immerse in Hawaiian Culture

Hawaii's charm extends far beyond its scenic splendor—it's a living testament to the rich tapestry of its indigenous culture. Take time to delve into the islands' history, visiting museums, and cultural centers that celebrate Hawaii's heritage. Attend a traditional luau to witness mesmerizing hula dances, feast on authentic Hawaiian fare, and experience the ancient art of fire dancing firsthand.

Cherish the Environment

As you explore Hawaii's natural wonders, it's crucial to tread lightly and honor the fragile ecosystem that sustains life here. Practice eco-conscious tourism—stay on designated paths, dispose of waste responsibly, and refrain from disturbing wildlife. By preserving Hawaii's pristine beauty, you play a vital role in safeguarding this paradise for future generations.

Revel in Relaxation

In the midst of Hawaii's natural splendor, find solace and rejuvenation for your mind, body, and soul. Treat yourself to a pampering spa session, practice yoga on the beach at sunrise, or simply unwind with a leisurely stroll along the shore. Let the rhythm of the islands wash over you, where time slows, and worries dissolve into the ether.

CHAPTER 2
UNDERSTANDING HAWAII

2.1 Geography, Climate and Best Time to Visit

Hawaii is a paradise for travelers seeking an escape from the ordinary. This archipelago consists of eight main islands, each offering its own unique charm and beauty. Understanding the geography, climate, and best times to visit Hawaii is essential for making the most of your experience in this enchanting destination.

Geography of Hawaii

Hawaii's geography is as diverse as it is stunning, characterized by volcanic peaks, lush rainforests, cascading waterfalls, and pristine beaches. The eight main islands that make up the state are Hawaii (also known as the Big Island), Maui, Oahu, Kauai, Molokai, Lanai, Niihau, and Kahoolawe. Each island boasts its own distinct topography and attractions, from the dramatic landscapes of the Big Island to the vibrant cultural scene of Oahu. Navigating Hawaii's geography requires careful planning, as each island offers a plethora of activities and sights to explore. Renting a car is often the most convenient way to get around, allowing you the flexibility to explore at your own pace. Alternatively, guided tours and public transportation options are available for those who prefer not to drive.

Climate of Hawaii

Hawaii enjoys a tropical climate characterized by warm temperatures year-round, making it an ideal destination for sun-seekers and outdoor enthusiasts. However, the weather can vary significantly depending on the island and the time of year.

Best Times to Visit Hawaii

Choosing the best time to visit Hawaii depends on your preferences and what you hope to experience during your trip. Generally, the islands experience two main seasons: the dry season (kau) and the wet season (hooilo).

Dry Season (Kau)

The dry season in Hawaii typically runs from April to October, offering visitors plenty of sunshine and minimal rainfall. This is considered the peak tourist season, as travelers flock to the islands to bask in the warm weather and enjoy outdoor activities such as snorkeling, hiking, and surfing. During the dry season, temperatures range from the mid-70s to the low 90s Fahrenheit, creating perfect conditions for exploring Hawaii's stunning beaches and natural wonders. However, it's important to note that the summer months (June to August) can be particularly crowded, so booking accommodations and activities in advance is advisable.

Wet Season (Hooilo)

The wet season in Hawaii typically occurs from November to March, bringing higher levels of rainfall and occasionally cooler temperatures. While this may deter some visitors, the wet season also has its advantages, including fewer crowds and lower prices on accommodations and activities. Despite the increased rainfall, Hawaii's wet season still offers plenty of opportunities for exploration and adventure. The lush vegetation thrives during this time, creating vibrant landscapes and cascading waterfalls. Plus, the occasional rain showers provide relief from the heat and add an element of tropical romance to the atmosphere.

Navigating the Weather

Regardless of when you visit Hawaii, it's important to be prepared for the possibility of changing weather conditions. Packing lightweight, breathable clothing, sunscreen, and a waterproof jacket is essential, as is staying hydrated and protecting yourself from the sun's rays. When planning outdoor activities, keep an eye on the weather forecast and be flexible with your itinerary. If rain is in the forecast, consider exploring indoor attractions such as museums, galleries, and cultural sites, or simply relax and enjoy the slower pace of island life.

2.2 History and Culture

The origins of Hawaii are shrouded in the mists of time, tracing back to the Polynesian voyagers who braved the vast expanse of the Pacific Ocean in sturdy canoes. These intrepid navigators, guided only by the stars and the currents, arrived on the shores of Hawaii centuries ago, carrying with them the seeds of a culture that would blossom into something truly extraordinary. Stepping foot on the sacred land of Hawaii, one cannot help but feel the palpable connection to its storied past. From the towering peaks of Mauna Kea to the lush valleys of Waimea, every inch of this island chain is steeped in history. The ancient Hawaiian people, with their deep reverence for the land and sea, left behind a legacy that continues to shape the cultural tapestry of Hawaii to this day.

One of the most iconic symbols of Hawaiian culture is the hula, a graceful dance that tells stories of love, nature, and mythology. Passed down through generations, the hula embodies the spirit of aloha, a philosophy of love, compassion, and respect for all living things. As the rhythmic chants and swaying movements transport you to a world of enchantment, you can't help but be drawn into the captivating allure of Hawaii's cultural heritage. But Hawaii's cultural richness extends far beyond the realm of dance and music. The islands are home to a wealth of sacred sites, each holding its own significance in Hawaiian mythology. From the towering cliffs of the Na Pali Coast to the volcanic landscapes of Hawaii Volcanoes National Park, these sacred places serve as reminders of the deep spiritual connection that the Hawaiian people have with their land.

As you wander through the ancient temples and heiaus scattered across the islands, you can't help but feel a sense of awe at the ingenuity of Hawaii's ancestors. These masterful architects and engineers built monumental structures without the aid of modern technology, using only the resources that the land provided. Their legacy stands as a testament to the resilience and creativity of the Hawaiian people. But perhaps the greatest treasure of Hawaii lies in its people. Warm and welcoming, they embody the spirit of aloha in everything they do. Whether you're sharing a meal of freshly caught fish with a local family or learning the art of lei-making from a master craftsman, you'll be embraced as ohana, or family.

2.3 Language, Communication & Essential Hawaiian Phrases
Hawaii is a melting pot of cultures, and its linguistic diversity reflects this rich tapestry. While English is widely spoken and understood throughout the islands, you'll also encounter Hawaiian, which holds a special place in the hearts of locals as the indigenous language of the archipelago. Additionally, due to its status as a popular tourist destination, you'll find that many residents are proficient in other languages, such as Japanese, Chinese, and Spanish. Embrace this linguistic mosaic as you embark on your Hawaiian adventure.

Key Phrases for Everyday Communication
While most Hawaiians are fluent in English, incorporating a few Hawaiian phrases into your conversations can enhance your cultural experience and foster connections with the locals. Here are some useful phrases to add a touch of aloha to your interactions:

Aloha (ah-LOH-hah) - The ubiquitous Hawaiian greeting, meaning hello, goodbye, and love.

Mahalo (mah-HAH-loh) - Thank you. Express gratitude with this essential phrase.

E komo mai (eh KOH-moh my) - Welcome. Extend a warm invitation or express appreciation for being welcomed.

Ohana (oh-HAH-nah) - Family. Acknowledge the importance of family and community in Hawaiian culture.

Hau'oli (how-OH-lee) - Happy. Share joy and well-wishes with this uplifting word.

Navigating Conversational Etiquette

In Hawaii, communication is infused with the spirit of aloha—warmth, kindness, and respect. When engaging in conversations, remember to:

Be courteous and attentive, actively listening to others and maintaining eye contact.

Use a friendly and respectful tone, addressing people with honorifics like "Aunty" or "Uncle" for elders, and "Brother" or "Sister" for peers.

Embrace the laid-back vibe of the islands, allowing conversations to unfold naturally without rushing or interrupting.

Cultural Sensitivity and Respect

As a visitor to Hawaii, it's essential to approach interactions with cultural sensitivity and respect. Here are some guidelines to keep in mind:

Avoid cultural appropriation by refraining from donning sacred attire or using cultural symbols without understanding their significance.

Respect personal space and boundaries, especially in crowded areas or during traditional ceremonies.

Learn about Hawaiian customs and traditions, showing genuine interest and appreciation for the local culture.

Navigating Language Barriers

In the rare event that you encounter language barriers during your stay in Hawaii, don't hesitate to seek assistance from locals, hotel staff, or tour guides. Many establishments, especially those frequented by tourists, offer multilingual support to accommodate visitors from diverse backgrounds. Additionally, carrying a pocket-sized phrasebook or using translation apps can be invaluable tools for overcoming linguistic challenges and facilitating communication.

2.4 Cultural Do's and Don'ts

Hawaii is not just a destination; it's a cultural experience that captivates the soul and leaves a lasting impression on all who visit. To truly immerse yourself in the aloha spirit and show respect for the local culture, it's essential to be mindful of certain cultural do's and don'ts during your time in the islands.

Respect Sacred Sites: Hawaii is home to numerous sacred sites, including heiaus (temples), burial grounds, and cultural landmarks. These places hold immense significance for the native Hawaiian people and should be treated with reverence and respect. When visiting sacred sites, follow any posted guidelines, refrain from touching or disturbing artifacts, and maintain a respectful demeanor at all times.

Participate in Cultural Activities: Immerse yourself in Hawaiian culture by participating in traditional activities and events. Attend a hula performance, learn to play the ukulele, or join a lei-making workshop to gain a deeper appreciation for the island's rich heritage. By engaging in cultural activities, you not only support local artisans and performers but also create meaningful connections with the community.

Practice Lonoikamakahiki: Lonoikamakahiki, or sharing and generosity, is a fundamental value in Hawaiian culture. Whether you're invited to a luau, sharing a meal with locals, or simply interacting with others, practice kindness and generosity in all your interactions. Offer to help others, share your experiences and knowledge, and express gratitude for the hospitality extended to you.

Show Respect for Nature: Hawaii's natural beauty is unparalleled, with pristine beaches, lush rainforests, and breathtaking landscapes at every turn. To honor the land and its inhabitants, practice responsible tourism and environmental stewardship during your visit. Dispose of trash properly, avoid damaging coral reefs and marine life while snorkeling or diving, and tread lightly on hiking trails to minimize your impact on the fragile ecosystem.

2.5 Tips for Interacting with Locals
When you visit Hawaii, you're not just exploring a destination; you're entering a vibrant tapestry of culture, tradition, and community. To truly immerse yourself in the aloha spirit and forge meaningful connections with the local people, it's essential to approach interactions with respect, curiosity, and an open heart.

Learn the Language: While English is widely spoken in Hawaii, learning a few words and phrases in Hawaiian can go a long way in building rapport with locals. Take the time to familiarize yourself with common greetings, expressions, and cultural terms, and don't be afraid to use them in your interactions. Locals will appreciate your effort to embrace their language and culture, and it will enhance your overall experience in the islands.

Respect Local Customs and Traditions: Hawaii has a rich cultural heritage that is deeply rooted in tradition and reverence for the land. To show respect for the local customs and traditions, familiarize yourself with basic etiquette guidelines and cultural practices. For example, remove your shoes before entering someone's home, offer a lei as a gesture of goodwill, and avoid touching sacred artifacts or sites without permission. By honoring these customs, you'll demonstrate your respect for the culture and earn the respect of the locals in return.

Support Local Businesses: Hawaii is home to a wealth of talented artisans, entrepreneurs, and small businesses that contribute to the unique fabric of the islands. Show your support for the local community by patronizing locally-owned shops, restaurants, and vendors. Whether you're savoring freshly caught seafood at a family-owned restaurant, browsing handmade crafts at a roadside market, or sipping on a refreshing shave ice from a neighborhood stand, your support helps to sustain the local economy and preserve the island's cultural heritage.

Engage in Meaningful Conversations: One of the best ways to connect with locals in Hawaii is through meaningful conversations. Take the time to engage in genuine dialogue with residents, whether it's striking up a conversation with a shopkeeper, chatting with your tour guide, or sharing stories with fellow travelers. Ask questions, listen attentively, and be curious about the experiences and perspectives of those you meet. By fostering open communication and mutual understanding, you'll forge lasting connections that enrich your travel experience.

Participate in Community Events: Hawaii is a place where community is valued and celebrated, and participating in local events and festivals is a great way to experience this sense of camaraderie firsthand. Attend a traditional hula performance, join a beach cleanup initiative, or volunteer at a cultural festival to connect with locals and immerse yourself in the vibrant tapestry of Hawaiian culture. By actively engaging with the community, you'll not only gain insight into the local way of life but also contribute to the preservation and celebration of Hawaiian heritage.

CHAPTER 3
PLANNING YOUR TRIP

3.1 Visa and Entry Requirements
Navigating the visa requirements and entry procedures to Hawaii is essential for any traveler looking to experience the beauty and culture of this Pacific paradise. Whether arriving by air, train, or road, understanding the entry process ensures a smooth and hassle-free journey.

Air Travel Entry Procedures
Arriving in Hawaii by air is the most common and convenient option for visitors from around the world. Before departure, travelers must ensure they meet the visa requirements for entry into the United States. Many nationalities are eligible for the Visa Waiver Program (VWP), allowing for visa-free travel to Hawaii for stays of up to 90 days. However, it's crucial to apply for an Electronic System for Travel Authorization (ESTA) online before boarding the flight to Hawaii. The ESTA serves as pre-screening for travelers from VWP

countries and must be approved before departure. Upon arrival at one of Hawaii's international airports, such as Honolulu International Airport or Kahului Airport, travelers will proceed through immigration and customs. Immigration officers will verify travel documents, including passports and ESTA approval. After clearing immigration, travelers collect their luggage and proceed through customs inspection. Visitors should declare any items subject to customs regulations, such as agricultural products or large sums of money.

Train Entry Procedures

While train travel to Hawaii is not possible due to its island geography, travelers can reach the islands by train within the United States before connecting to a flight or cruise ship. Major cities like Los Angeles and San Francisco serve as transportation hubs for travelers heading to Hawaii. Amtrak offers long-distance train services to these cities, providing a scenic journey through diverse landscapes. Upon reaching the mainland port city, travelers can transfer to a flight or cruise ship bound for Hawaii.

Road Entry Procedures

For travelers within the United States or neighboring countries like Canada and Mexico, reaching Hawaii by road involves a combination of driving and ferry or cruise ship transportation. Those driving to Hawaii typically begin their journey on the west coast of the United States, such as California. From there, travelers can drive to a port city like Los Angeles or San Diego to board a ferry or cruise ship bound for Hawaii. Alternatively, travelers can drive to a northern port city like Seattle or Vancouver and embark on a longer ocean voyage to Hawaii. Regardless of the mode of transportation, all visitors to Hawaii must adhere to entry procedures and customs regulations. Familiarizing oneself with visa requirements, obtaining necessary travel authorizations, and following immigration and customs procedures ensures a seamless and enjoyable experience exploring the enchanting islands of Hawaii. From the moment of arrival, travelers are greeted with the warm aloha spirit and the promise of unforgettable adventures amidst stunning natural beauty.

3.2 Health and Safety Tips

Before embarking on your journey to Hawaii, it's important to be aware of potential health risks associated with travel to the islands. While Hawaii is generally a safe destination for travelers, there are a few health concerns to keep in mind, including sun exposure, dehydration, and ocean-related injuries. Understanding these risks and taking preventative measures can help ensure a safe and enjoyable visit.

Sun Protection

Hawaii's tropical climate means plenty of sunshine year-round, but it also means increased exposure to harmful UV rays. To protect yourself from sunburn and reduce the risk of skin cancer, be sure to wear sunscreen with a high SPF rating, reapply it frequently (especially after swimming or sweating), and seek shade during the hottest hours of the day. Wearing a wide-brimmed hat, sunglasses, and lightweight clothing can also provide additional protection from the sun's rays.

Hydration

With its warm temperatures and high humidity, staying hydrated is crucial when visiting Hawaii. Drink plenty of water throughout the day, especially if you're engaging in outdoor activities such as hiking, swimming, or sightseeing. Avoid excessive alcohol consumption, as it can contribute to dehydration, and be mindful of your fluid intake, particularly if you're spending extended periods of time in the sun.

Ocean Safety

Hawaii's pristine beaches and crystal-clear waters are a major draw for visitors, but they can also pose risks for swimmers, surfers, and snorkelers. Before venturing into the ocean, familiarize yourself with local conditions, including wave heights, currents, and potential hazards such as coral reefs and rocky outcrops. Swim at lifeguarded beaches whenever possible, and always heed warning signs and flags indicating dangerous conditions. If you're not a strong swimmer, consider wearing a flotation device or staying in shallow waters where you can touch the bottom.

Mosquito Protection

While Hawaii is not known for mosquito-borne diseases such as malaria or Zika virus, mosquitoes can still be a nuisance, especially in certain areas and during certain times of the year. To protect yourself from mosquito bites, use insect repellent containing DEET or other EPA-approved ingredients, wear long sleeves and pants during dawn and dusk when mosquitoes are most active, and use screened windows and doors to keep mosquitoes out of your accommodations.

Medical Services

In the event of a medical emergency or illness during your visit to Hawaii, rest assured that the islands are equipped with modern medical facilities and qualified healthcare professionals. However, it's a good idea to familiarize yourself with the location of hospitals, urgent care centers, and pharmacies in your area, especially if you're staying in a more remote or rural area. Consider purchasing travel insurance that includes coverage for medical expenses and emergency evacuation, just in case.

3.3 Packing Essentials

Before packing for your trip to Hawaii, it's important to understand the climate and geography of the islands. Hawaii enjoys a tropical climate, with warm temperatures year-round and occasional rain showers, especially in the winter months. The islands are also known for their diverse landscapes, ranging from pristine beaches and lush rainforests to volcanic peaks and cascading waterfalls. By taking these factors into account, you can ensure that you pack appropriately for your Hawaiian adventure.

Clothing

When it comes to clothing, lightweight and breathable fabrics are key for staying cool and comfortable in Hawaii's warm and humid climate. Pack a variety of outfits suitable for beach days, outdoor adventures, and casual dining. Don't forget to include swimwear, flip-flops or sandals, a wide-brimmed hat, sunglasses, and a light jacket or sweater for cooler evenings or higher elevations. If you plan on hiking or exploring rugged terrain, sturdy closed-toe shoes are essential for safety and support.

Outdoor Gear

Hawaii offers endless opportunities for outdoor adventure, from snorkeling and surfing to hiking and zip-lining. Depending on your planned activities, consider packing gear such as snorkel gear, water shoes, a beach umbrella or shade tent, and a waterproof phone case or dry bag for protecting valuables while on the water. If you plan on hiking, be sure to pack a daypack with essentials such as water, snacks, a map or GPS device, a first-aid kit, and a flashlight or headlamp.

Miscellaneous Items

In addition to clothing and gear, there are a few miscellaneous items that can come in handy during your trip to Hawaii. Pack a reusable water bottle to stay hydrated on the go, as well as a travel-sized hand sanitizer for times when handwashing facilities are not readily available. Don't forget to bring any necessary medications or medical supplies, as well as a copy of your prescription in case you need to refill medications while on the islands. Lastly, consider packing a small backpack or tote bag for day trips and outings, as well as a camera or smartphone to capture memories of your Hawaiian adventure.

3.4 Currency Exchange and Budgeting for Your Trip

When planning a visit to Hawaii, understanding the currency, banking services, and budgeting options is essential for a smooth and enjoyable trip. Hawaii, as part of the United States, uses the US dollar (USD) as its official currency. Visitors should be aware of the current exchange rates and plan their budgets accordingly.

Banking Services

Hawaii boasts a range of banking institutions offering various services to meet the needs of visitors. Five prominent banks in Hawaii include Bank of Hawaii, First Hawaiian Bank, American Savings Bank, Central Pacific Bank, and Hawaii National Bank. Each bank provides a range of services, including currency exchange, ATM access, and international wire transfers.

Bank of Hawaii: With branches located throughout the islands, Bank of Hawaii offers convenient banking services for visitors. Travelers can access ATMs for cash withdrawals and currency exchange services at select locations. The bank also provides online banking options for managing finances on the go.

First Hawaiian Bank: As one of the largest banks in Hawaii, First Hawaiian Bank serves both residents and visitors with a wide range of banking services. Travelers can utilize the bank's ATMs for cash withdrawals and currency exchange services. First Hawaiian Bank also offers international banking services for travelers requiring assistance with foreign transactions.

American Savings Bank: Another prominent banking institution in Hawaii, American Savings Bank, provides comprehensive banking services for visitors. Travelers can access ATMs conveniently located across the islands and take advantage of currency exchange services at select branches. The bank also offers online banking options for easy money management.

Central Pacific Bank: Serving the community for over 60 years, Central Pacific Bank offers personalized banking services for visitors to Hawaii. Travelers can find ATMs at various locations for cash withdrawals and utilize currency exchange services at select branches. Central Pacific Bank also provides international banking solutions for travelers' financial needs.

Hawaii National Bank: With a focus on customer service and community involvement, Hawaii National Bank offers banking services tailored to visitors' needs. Travelers can access ATMs for cash withdrawals and currency exchange services at select branches. The bank also provides online banking options for convenient account management.

Currency Exchange Bureau

For visitors in need of currency exchange services, Hawaii offers several options throughout the islands. Popular locations include airports, major hotels, and tourist areas. Visitors can also find currency exchange bureaus at shopping centers and financial institutions in urban areas like Honolulu and Waikiki. Additionally, many banks mentioned above offer currency exchange services at select branches, providing travelers with convenient access to funds in the local currency.

3.5 Accommodation Options

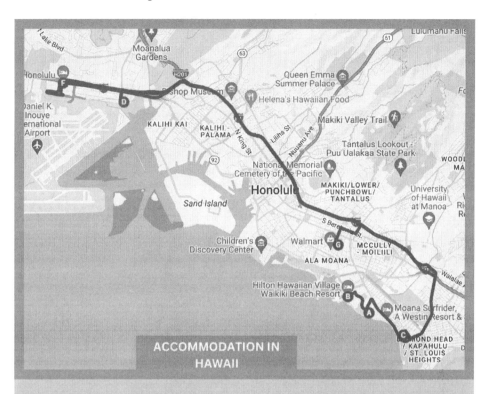

Directions from Halekulani Hotel, Kālia Road, Honolulu, HI, USA to Pagoda Hotel, Rycroft Street, Honolulu, HI, USA

A
Halekulani Hotel, Kālia Road, Honolulu, HI, USA

B
Hilton Hawaiian Village Waikiki Beach Resort, Kālia Road, Honolulu, HI, USA

C
Waikiki Beachside Hostel, Lemon Road, Honolulu, HI, USA

D
Pacific Marina Inn, Waiwai Loop, Honolulu, HI, USA

E
Polynesian Hostel Beach Club, Lemon Road, Honolulu, HI, USA

F
Airport Honolulu Hotel North Nimitz Higsway, Honolulu, HI USA

G
Pagoda Hotel Rycroft Street, Honolulu, HI USA

Hawaii, an idyllic paradise known for its stunning landscapes, rich cultural heritage, and vibrant hospitality industry, offers a wide range of accommodation options to suit every traveler's needs. From luxurious beachfront resorts to budget-friendly hostels, and from unique stays to cozy vacation rentals, Hawaii's lodging landscape is as diverse as its natural beauty. This guide explores various accommodation choices across the Hawaiian Islands, detailing their locations, amenities, prices, and unique features to help visitors make informed decisions for their dream vacation.

Luxury Hotels:

Halekulani Hotel

Located in the heart of Waikiki, Halekulani Hotel is the epitome of luxury and elegance. This five-star hotel offers breathtaking views of Diamond Head and Waikiki Beach. Rooms are spacious, with prices starting at $700 per night. Guests can indulge in fine dining at the hotel's renowned restaurants, such as La Mer, or relax in the serene SpaHalekulani. The hotel also offers a range of special services, including personalized guest experiences and exclusive cultural programs. More information and reservations can be made at (https://www.halekulani.com).

Hilton Hawaiian Village Waikiki Beach Resort

Situated on 22 acres of lush tropical gardens, the Hilton Hawaiian Village Waikiki Beach Resort offers an unparalleled beachfront experience. With prices starting at $300 per night, this resort features multiple pools, a private lagoon, and a variety of dining options. Unique amenities include the Mandara Spa and the Waikiki Starlight Luau. The resort's Rainbow Tower provides stunning ocean views, and its central location offers easy access to Waikiki's attractions. For bookings, visit (https://www.hiltonhawaiianvillage.com).

Royal Kona Resort

Located on the picturesque Kona Coast, the Royal Kona Resort offers a blend of comfort and tradition. Prices start at $180 per night. The resort features an oceanfront pool, spa services, and a private lagoon for snorkeling. Don the Beachcomber, the on-site restaurant, serves delicious Hawaiian cuisine. Guests can also enjoy the Legends of Hawaii Luau, an authentic Polynesian cultural experience. For more details, visit (https://www.royalkona.com).

Turtle Bay Resort

Turtle Bay Resort offers a secluded and luxurious escape. With rooms starting at $400 per night, the resort boasts two championship golf courses, a full-service spa, and seven restaurants. Unique features include horseback riding along the beach and surf lessons at the Turtle Bay Surf School. The resort's location provides easy access to some of Hawaii's best surf spots and scenic hikes. For reservations, go to (https://www.turtlebayresort.com).

Budget Accommodations

Pagoda Hotel

Situated in Honolulu, Pagoda Hotel offers affordable accommodations with rates starting at $120 per night. It features a unique koi pond and garden, a swimming pool, and an on-site restaurant. Its central location is ideal for exploring Honolulu. For bookings, check [Pagoda Hotel](#).

Pacific Marina Inn

Conveniently located near Honolulu International Airport, Pacific Marina Inn offers budget-friendly accommodation starting at $130 per night. The hotel features an outdoor pool, a restaurant, and free 24-hour airport shuttle service. It's ideal for travelers with early or late flights and provides easy access to downtown Honolulu. For more information, visit (https://www.pacificmarinainn.com).

Wild Ginger Hotel

Situated in Hilo, the Wild Ginger Hotel offers a charming and affordable stay with rates starting at $90 per night. This quaint hotel provides a tropical garden setting, complimentary breakfast, and easy access to Hilo's attractions like the Rainbow Falls and Liliuokalani Gardens. It's perfect for those looking to explore the natural beauty of the Big Island on a budget. More details can be found at (https://www.wildgingerhotel.com).

Hilo Reeds Bay Hotel

Also in Hilo, the Hilo Reeds Bay Hotel offers budget accommodation with prices starting at $95 per night. This hotel features oceanfront views, a swimming pool, and kitchenettes in some rooms, making it suitable for longer stays. Its location near Hilo Bay provides easy access to local attractions and the Hawaii Volcanoes National Park. For reservations, visit (https://www.hiloreedsbayhotel.com).

Vacation Homes and Rentals

Maui Seaside Hotel

Located in Kahului, Maui Seaside Hotel offers comfortable rooms and suites with prices starting at $180 per night. This family-owned hotel features a pool, beachfront access, and an on-site restaurant, Tante's Island Cuisine. It's an excellent choice for families and travelers looking for a home-like atmosphere with the convenience of hotel amenities. Bookings can be made at (https://www.mauiseasidehotel.com).

Waimea Country Lodge

For a rustic and peaceful retreat, Waimea Country Lodge on the Big Island offers cozy accommodations starting at $120 per night. The lodge provides a serene environment with stunning views of Mauna Kea and easy access to the Parker Ranch. It's ideal for visitors looking to experience Hawaii's countryside and outdoor activities. More information is available at (https://www.waimeacountrylodge.com).

Unique Stays:

Hotel Molokai

Hotel Molokai offers a unique Polynesian-style experience with rates starting at $200 per night. Located on the island of Molokai, this boutique hotel features thatched-roof bungalows, an oceanfront pool, and live Hawaiian music at the on-site restaurant, Hula Shores. Guests can enjoy a truly local experience and explore the unspoiled beauty of Molokai. For bookings, visit (https://www.hotelmolokai.com).

Polynesian Hostel Beach Club

Situated in Waikiki, the Polynesian Hostel Beach Club provides a vibrant and social atmosphere for travelers with rates starting at $50 per night for a dormitory bed. The hostel offers free breakfast, organized tours, and activities such as surfing and hiking. It's a great option for young travelers and those looking to experience the lively Waikiki scene on a budget. For more information, visit (https://www.polynesianhostel.com).

Airport Honolulu Hotel

For travelers needing convenient access to Honolulu International Airport, the Airport Honolulu Hotel offers comfortable accommodations starting at $160 per night. The hotel features a 24-hour airport shuttle, an outdoor pool, and a restaurant. It's ideal for business travelers and those with layovers. More details can be found at (https://www.airporthonoluluhotel.com).

3.6 Getting to Hawaii

Embarking on a journey to Hawaii promises an unforgettable adventure filled with stunning landscapes, vibrant culture, and warm hospitality. Whether you're drawn to the pristine beaches of Waikiki, the lush rainforests of Kauai, or the volcanic wonders of the Big Island, getting to this Pacific paradise is the first step in your memorable experience.

By Air

Air travel remains the most popular and convenient mode of transportation to Hawaii, offering a multitude of options to suit every traveler's preferences and budget. Numerous airlines operate flights to the islands, including major carriers like Hawaiian Airlines (https://www.hawaiianairlines.com/), United Airlines (https://www.united.com/), American Airlines (https://www.aa.com/), Delta Air Lines (https://www.delta.com/), and Alaska Airlines (https://www.alaskaair.com/), ensuring ample choices for visitors from around the globe. When it comes to booking flights, flexibility is key to securing the best deals. Utilizing online travel agencies such as Expedia, Kayak, or Skyscanner allows you to compare prices across multiple airlines and find the most competitive fares. Additionally, subscribing to airline newsletters or following them on social media can provide access to exclusive discounts and promotions.

While prices can vary depending on factors such as travel dates, departure city, and demand, the average cost of a round-trip ticket to Hawaii from the mainland United States typically ranges from $400 to $800, with fluctuations throughout the year. Booking in advance and considering alternative airports or travel dates can help mitigate expenses. For those seeking a more luxurious and personalized experience, premium cabin options and first-class upgrades offer enhanced comfort and amenities, albeit at a higher price point. However, the breathtaking views of the Pacific Ocean and the anticipation of your Hawaiian getaway make the journey itself a part of the adventure.

By Train

Although Hawaii lacks a traditional railway system due to its island geography, visitors can still embark on a unique train journey on the island of Oahu. The historic and iconic Oahu Railway & Land Company, known as the Hawaiian Railway Society (https://www.hawaiianrailway.com/), operates scenic excursions aboard vintage trains, providing passengers with a nostalgic glimpse into Hawaii's past. Travelers can board the train at the Ewa Railroad Station in Oahu's countryside and embark on a leisurely ride along the island's picturesque coastline, passing through charming towns, verdant landscapes, and historic sites along the way. With open-air seating and knowledgeable guides narrating the journey, the experience offers a delightful blend of relaxation and exploration.

Tickets for the Oahu Railway & Land Company's excursions can be purchased online through their official website or at the station ticket office, with prices typically ranging from $20 to $40 per person depending on the chosen route and class of service. Reservations are recommended, especially during peak tourist seasons, to secure your preferred departure time and seating arrangements.

By Road

For intrepid adventurers eager to explore Hawaii at their own pace, road travel presents an exhilarating opportunity to uncover hidden gems and breathtaking vistas across the islands. Renting a car upon arrival at one of Hawaii's major airports, such as Honolulu International Airport on Oahu or Kahului Airport on Maui, allows you the freedom to traverse scenic highways and rugged terrain with ease. Major car rental companies, including Enterprise, Hertz, Avis, and Budget, operate branches throughout Hawaii, offering a wide selection of vehicles ranging from compact cars to SUVs and luxury sedans. Advance reservations are recommended, especially during peak travel periods, to ensure availability and secure competitive rates.

Navigating Hawaii's well-maintained road network is relatively straightforward, with major highways connecting key destinations and attractions on each island. However, it's essential to familiarize yourself with local traffic laws, road signs, and driving conditions, particularly if you're accustomed to driving on the opposite side of the road. As you embark on your road trip adventure, be sure to embrace spontaneity and allow ample time for detours and unexpected discoveries along the way. From the winding road to Hana on Maui to the scenic drive along the Kona coast on the Big Island, each route offers its own unique blend of natural beauty and cultural richness, inviting you to immerse yourself in the spirit of aloha.

3.7 Transportation Options

When traversing the enchanting islands of Hawaii, visitors are met with a myriad of transportation options, catering to diverse preferences and budgets. From well-established public transportation systems to convenient ride-sharing services, Hawaii offers a range of choices for getting around its beautiful landscapes. Let's delve into the various modes of transportation available across the islands.

-TheBus (Oahu): TheBus provides extensive coverage across Oahu, including popular tourist destinations such as Waikiki, Pearl Harbor, and Diamond Head. Visitors can find route maps, schedules, and fare information on the official website: (https://www.thebus.org/).

-Maui Bus (Maui): Operated by the County of Maui Department of Transportation, the Maui Bus offers routes covering key areas like Lahaina,

Kihei, and Kahului. Information on routes, schedules, and fares can be found on the official website: (https://shorturl.at/YInpd).

-Kauai Bus (Kauai): The Kauai Bus serves Kauai Island, providing routes connecting major towns and attractions. Visitors can access route maps, schedules, and fare details on the official website: (https://www.kauai.gov/Transportation).

-Hele-On Bus (Hawaii Island): Hele-On Bus offers transportation across Hawaii Island at affordable rates. Information on routes, schedules, and fares can be found on the official website: (https://www.heleonbus.org/).

Taxi Companies and Ride-Sharing Services

-Charley's Taxi (Oahu): Charley's Taxi provides traditional taxi services on Oahu. Visitors can book taxis and find fare information on the official website: (https://charleystaxi.com/).

-TheCAB (Oahu): TheCAB operates taxi services on Oahu with metered fares. Information on booking taxis and fare rates can be found on the official website: (https://www.thecabhawaii.com/).

-Uber: Uber operates ride-sharing services on all major islands in Hawaii. Visitors can request rides through the Uber app (*available on google playstore and applestore*) and find fare estimates based on their destination and route.

-Lyft: Lyft offers ride-sharing services across Hawaii, allowing visitors to request rides conveniently through the Lyft app. Fare estimates and ride options are available on the official website: (https://www.lyft.com/rider/cities/honolulu-hi).

Biking and Cycling Routes

-Hawaii Bicycling League: The Hawaii Bicycling League website provides information on cycling routes, safety tips, and upcoming events for cyclists across the islands: (https://www.hbl.org/).

Car Rental Companies

-Enterprise: Enterprise Rent-A-Car offers a wide range of vehicles for rent on the Hawaiian Islands. Visitors can book rental cars and find information on rates and locations on the official website: (https://shorturl.at/Trg5Q).

-Hertz: Hertz Car Rental operates across Hawaii, providing rental vehicles ranging from compact cars to SUVs and luxury vehicles. Rental bookings and information on rates can be found on the official website: (https://www.hertz.com/rentacar/reservation/).

-Avis: Avis Car Rental offers rental services on the Hawaiian Islands, with a variety of vehicles available for tourists. Visitors can book rental cars and find rental locations on the official website: (https://www.avis.com/en/locations/us/hi).

-Discount Hawaii Car Rental: Discount Hawaii Car Rental provides rental car services at competitive rates across Hawaii. Visitors can book rental vehicles and find special deals on the official website: (https://www.discounthawaiicarrental.com/).

-Paradise Rent-A-Car: Paradise Rent-A-Car is a local car rental company operating in Hawaii. Visitors can rent vehicles and find information on rates and locations on the official website: (https://www.paradiserentals.com/).

Navigating Effectively

To navigate effectively in Hawaii, visitors can utilize the information provided on the respective websites of transportation companies. Additionally, tourist information centers and hotel concierge services can offer assistance in planning transportation options and itineraries. By leveraging the diverse transportation infrastructure of Hawaii and utilizing online resources, visitors can explore the islands with ease and convenience.

CHAPTER 4
EXPLORING OAHU

4.1 Overview of Oahu

The story of Oahu begins in the mists of ancient Polynesian navigation, where daring voyagers from the Marquesas Islands first set foot on its shores around 300 AD. These early settlers were guided by the stars and driven by a spirit of exploration, bringing with them a profound respect for nature and a sophisticated system of sustainable living. They established a society deeply intertwined with the land and sea, cultivating taro in lush valleys and fishing in the bountiful waters. Centuries later, around 1000 AD, a second wave of Polynesians from Tahiti arrived, bringing new traditions and integrating with the existing communities. This period saw the rise of a complex social structure ruled by ali'i (chiefs) and governed by a strict kapu system, which dictated the spiritual and social order. The ali'i established powerful chiefdoms, and Oahu became a significant political and cultural center in the Hawaiian archipelago.

One of the most intriguing figures in Oahu's history is Kamehameha the Great, a warrior king from the Big Island who sought to unite the Hawaiian Islands. In 1795, after a series of fierce battles, including the pivotal Battle of Nuʻuanu, Kamehameha conquered Oahu, solidifying his control over the islands and ushering in a new era of unified Hawaiian Kingdom. The arrival of Western explorers in the late 18th century, notably Captain James Cook in 1778, marked the beginning of profound changes for Oahu. The island soon became a key port for whalers, traders, and eventually missionaries who introduced Christianity and Western education. This period also saw the tragic decline of the native Hawaiian population due to introduced diseases.

The 19th century brought significant economic transformation with the establishment of sugar and pineapple plantations. Immigrant labor from China, Japan, Portugal, and the Philippines contributed to Oahu's cultural melting pot, shaping its unique multicultural identity. The strategic importance of Oahu was recognized by the United States, leading to the annexation of Hawaii in 1898 and the establishment of Pearl Harbor as a major naval base. The bombing of Pearl Harbor on December 7, 1941, was a defining moment in Oahu's history, propelling the United States into World War II and leaving an indelible mark on the island. Today, Pearl Harbor stands as a poignant reminder of the sacrifices made, attracting millions of visitors to its memorials and museums.

In the decades following the war, Oahu blossomed into a modern metropolis. Honolulu, with its iconic Waikiki Beach, became a world-renowned tourist destination. The city offers a vibrant mix of luxury resorts, bustling markets, and a thriving arts scene. Yet, amidst this urban sprawl, the spirit of aloha endures, rooted in the island's ancient traditions and natural splendor. Oahu's landscape is a testament to its volcanic origins, featuring dramatic mountain ranges, verdant rainforests, and pristine beaches. The North Shore is famous for its towering surf, attracting surfers from around the globe, while the tranquil eastern coast boasts scenic vistas like Hanauma Bay and the Nuuanu Pali Lookout. Beyond its physical beauty, Oahu's true allure lies in its people and their stories. The island is a living tapestry of cultures, where hula dancers keep the ancient traditions alive, and local farmers share the bounty of the land at vibrant farmers' markets. The spirit of aloha, embodying love, compassion, and respect, is palpable in everyday interactions, inviting visitors to not just witness, but experience the essence of Hawaii.

4.2 Must-See Attractions

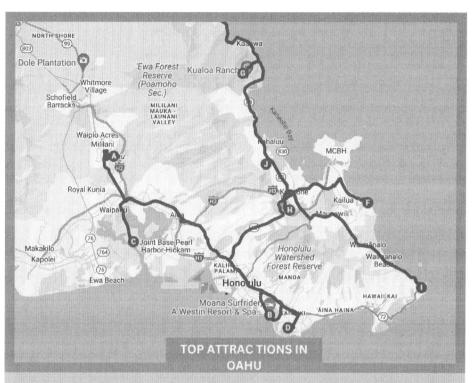

Directions from Oahu, Hawaii, USA to Byodo-In Temple, Kahekili Highway, Kaneohe, HI, USA

A Oahu, Hawaii, USA	D Diamond Head Crater Hike, Kapahulu, Honolulu, HI, USA	G Ho'omaluhia Botanical Garden, Luluku Rd, Kaneohe, HI, USA
B Waikiki Beach, Honolulu, HI, USA	E Lanikai Beach, Kailua, HI, USA	H Makapu'u Tide Pools, Honolulu, HI, USA
C Pearl Harbor, Hawaii, USA	F Kualoa Ranch, Kaneohe, HI, USA	I Byodo-In Temple, Kahekili Highway, Kaneohe, HI, USA

Oahu, the enchanting heart of Hawaii, is a paradise that beckons travelers with its stunning landscapes, vibrant culture, and profound history. Known as "The Gathering Place," Oahu offers a captivating blend of ancient traditions and modern allure, making it a destination like no other. Whether you're drawn by the allure of its pristine beaches, the echoes of its storied past, or the warmth of its diverse community, Oahu promises an experience that is both enriching and unforgettable. Here, we delve into must-visit attractions that encapsulate the essence of this extraordinary island: Waikiki Beach, Pearl Harbor, Diamond Head Crater, and the Polynesian Cultural Center. Each of these locations offers a unique glimpse into the multifaceted beauty of Oahu, ensuring that every moment spent here leaves a lasting impression. Each site tells a story, inviting visitors to delve deeper into the island's rich history and vibrant present. Whether you're exploring ancient trails, paying tribute to historical landmarks, or simply enjoying the sun and sea, Oahu promises a journey that will leave you enchanted and inspired.

- 4.2.1 Waikiki Beach

Waikiki Beach is a world-renowned stretch of golden sand that has become synonymous with the Hawaiian vacation experience. This iconic beach, framed by the turquoise waters of the Pacific Ocean, is more than just a picturesque spot for sunbathing; it's a vibrant cultural and recreational hub with something for everyone. To reach Waikiki Beach, visitors can easily access it from Honolulu International Airport via a short 20-minute drive. Public transportation options, such as TheBus, provide convenient routes to the beach from various parts of the island. The area is also highly walkable, with numerous hotels, shops, and dining establishments lining Kalakaua Avenue, the main thoroughfare.

Waikiki is the perfect place to embrace the aloha spirit and engage in water sports. The calm waters are ideal for swimming, paddleboarding, and snorkeling, providing a safe and enjoyable environment for visitors of all ages. Historically, Waikiki Beach was a retreat for Hawaiian royalty, who enjoyed its tranquil beauty and abundance of resources. Today, it continues to exude a regal charm, inviting visitors to explore its history at nearby landmarks like the statue of Duke Kahanamoku, the father of modern surfing. The Royal Hawaiian and Moana Surfrider hotels, both historic landmarks, offer a glimpse into the island's storied past.

In the evenings, Waikiki transforms into a lively hotspot with vibrant nightlife. Beachfront luaus, live music performances, and traditional hula shows offer a taste of Hawaiian culture and entertainment. Dining options range from casual beachside cafes to high-end restaurants, ensuring that every palate is satisfied. For those seeking retail therapy, the Waikiki Shopping Plaza and International Market Place offer a plethora of options, from luxury brands to unique local crafts.

- 4.2.2 Pearl Harbor

A visit to Oahu would be incomplete without a trip to Pearl Harbor, a site of profound historical significance that draws millions of visitors each year. Located on the island's southern coast, Pearl Harbor is approximately a

30-minute drive from Waikiki and is accessible by public transportation, including TheBus, which offers direct routes to the memorial. Pearl Harbor, the site of the infamous attack on December 7, 1941, which led the United States into World War II, stands today as a solemn reminder of the sacrifices made during the war. The Pearl Harbor National Memorial, including the USS Arizona Memorial, offers free entry, though reservations are recommended for specific tours and experiences. Upon arrival, visitors can start at the Pearl Harbor Visitor Center, where they can explore interactive exhibits and watch a documentary film detailing the events of the attack. A shuttle boat ride takes visitors to the USS Arizona Memorial, which floats above the sunken battleship and serves as a poignant tribute to the lives lost.

Other notable sites within Pearl Harbor include the Battleship Missouri Memorial, where the official surrender of Japan took place, and the USS Bowfin Submarine Museum & Park, which offers a glimpse into life aboard a World War II-era submarine. Each site offers guided tours and exhibits that provide a deeper understanding of the historical context and significance of Pearl Harbor. For aviation enthusiasts, the Pacific Aviation Museum showcases a collection of vintage aircraft and exhibits detailing the role of air power in the Pacific Theater. The museum is housed in historic hangars that withstood the attack, adding to the immersive experience. Visiting Pearl Harbor is a deeply moving experience, allowing visitors to pay their respects and gain a greater appreciation for the resilience and courage displayed during one of the most pivotal moments in history.

- 4.2.3 Diamond Head Crater

Dominating the Honolulu skyline, Diamond Head Crater, known as Lēʻahi in Hawaiian, is a must-see natural landmark that offers breathtaking panoramic views and a challenging yet rewarding hike. Located just a few miles from Waikiki, Diamond Head can be reached by car, public transportation, or even a leisurely bike ride along the scenic coastline. The hike to the summit is about 1.6 miles round trip, taking most visitors between 1.5 to 2 hours to complete. The trail, although steep and strenuous in parts, is well-maintained and suitable for most fitness levels, with plenty of rest stops along the way. Diamond Head's formation dates back over 300,000 years, originating from a volcanic eruption that created its distinctive saucer-shaped profile. Historically, the crater served as a strategic military lookout, with bunkers and observation posts still visible along the trail. Hikers can explore these remnants and learn about the crater's military significance through informational plaques.

At the summit, hikers are rewarded with stunning vistas of Waikiki, Honolulu, and the expansive Pacific Ocean. The views are particularly enchanting at sunrise and sunset, when the light casts a golden hue over the landscape. It's a perfect spot for photography, relaxation, and soaking in the natural beauty of Oahu. For those less inclined to hike, the base of Diamond Head offers other attractions, including the Kapiolani Community College Farmers' Market, where visitors can sample local produce and delicacies. Nearby, the Diamond Head Lighthouse, an active aid to navigation, stands as another picturesque landmark, adding to the charm of the area.

- 4.2.4 Polynesian Cultural Center

Immerse yourself in the rich tapestry of Pacific Island cultures at the Polynesian Cultural Center (PCC), located on the northeastern shore of Oahu in Laie. About an hour's drive from Waikiki, the PCC is accessible by car, and various tour operators offer shuttle services from major hotels. The Polynesian Cultural Center is a living museum and cultural theme park that celebrates the diverse traditions of Polynesia. Opened in 1963, the center spans 42 acres and features six authentic villages representing the islands of Hawaii, Samoa, Tahiti, Tonga, Fiji, and Aotearoa (New Zealand). Each village offers interactive demonstrations, performances, and hands-on activities, providing a unique and engaging way to learn about the customs, crafts, and lifestyles of these vibrant cultures. Admission to the PCC varies based on the package, with options including village tours, cultural presentations, and the renowned evening show, "Hā: Breath of Life." One of the highlights of a visit is the luau, a traditional Hawaiian feast that includes an array of local dishes such as kalua pig, poi, and haupia, accompanied by music and hula dancing.

The PCC also features the Hawaiian Journey Theater, where visitors can experience a cinematic presentation that takes them on a virtual tour of Hawaii's natural beauty and cultural heritage. For those interested in Polynesian art, the center houses a gallery showcasing intricate wood carvings, traditional textiles, and other artifacts. A visit to the Polynesian Cultural Center is not only educational but also deeply enriching, offering a profound appreciation for the cultural diversity and shared heritage of the Pacific Islands. The center's mission of preserving and promoting Polynesian culture ensures that every visitor leaves with a deeper understanding and respect for these ancient traditions.

4.3 Hidden Gems of Oahu

When you think of Oahu, iconic destinations like Waikiki Beach, Pearl Harbor, and Diamond Head Crater might immediately come to mind. However, beyond these well-trodden paths lie hidden gems that offer a more intimate glimpse into the island's soul. These secret spots are where the true magic of Oahu can be found, offering serene escapes, thrilling adventures, and authentic cultural experiences that will leave you enchanted and longing for more.

Lanikai Beach
Tucked away in the charming town of Kailua on Oahu's windward coast, Lanikai Beach is a slice of paradise that feels worlds away from the bustling city. Often overshadowed by its more famous counterparts, Lanikai offers pristine white sand and crystal-clear turquoise waters, making it a perfect spot for a tranquil retreat. The name "Lanikai" means "heavenly sea," and it's easy to see why. With its calm, gentle waves and stunning views of the Mokulua Islands, Lanikai Beach is ideal for swimming, kayaking, and snorkeling. To get there, it's a scenic 30-minute drive from Honolulu, but parking can be challenging as there are no public lots, so it's best to arrive early. Once you step onto the powdery sand, the effort feels worthwhile. Watching the sunrise at Lanikai is an ethereal experience, painting the sky in shades of pink and gold and casting a serene glow over the tranquil waters. For those who love a bit of adventure, a kayak trip to the nearby Mokulua Islands offers a chance to explore seabird sanctuaries and hidden tide pools.

Kualoa Ranch

For those seeking both adventure and history, Kualoa Ranch is an extraordinary destination nestled on Oahu's northeastern coast. This 4,000-acre private nature reserve and working cattle ranch is not only a place of breathtaking beauty but also rich cultural significance. It has been preserved by the same family for over 160 years and remains a testament to Hawaii's natural and historical heritage. The ranch offers a variety of tours and activities that cater to all interests. Movie buffs will thrill at the Hollywood Movie Sites Tour, which showcases filming locations for blockbusters like "Jurassic Park" and "Lost." For those craving adventure, options include ATV tours, ziplining, and horseback riding through lush valleys and along dramatic cliffs. Each tour is steeped in the history and mythology of the land, adding depth to the experience. Kualoa Ranch also holds the sacred Ka'a'awa Valley, known as "the Backlot of Hawaii," where you can explore ancient Hawaiian fishponds and gardens. The Legends of Kualoa tour delves into the ranch's cultural past, sharing stories of the area's significance to the native Hawaiian people.

Ho'omaluhia Botanical Garden

For a peaceful escape into nature, the Ho'omaluhia Botanical Garden in Kaneohe offers 400 acres of lush, landscaped beauty. Translating to "a place of peace and tranquility," Ho'omaluhia lives up to its name, providing a serene setting where visitors can reconnect with nature. This hidden gem is free to the public and open daily, making it an accessible oasis for those seeking a break from the hustle and bustle of city life. The garden features a vast array of tropical plants from around the world, organized by geographic regions such as Africa, Polynesia, and Hawaii. The tranquil lake at the center of the garden is perfect for a leisurely stroll, fishing (catch and release), or a relaxing picnic. Ho'omaluhia is also a haven for bird watchers and nature photographers, offering numerous scenic spots to capture the breathtaking landscapes. The garden hosts educational programs and guided tours that provide insights into the diverse flora and the efforts to preserve these natural treasures.

Makapu'u Tide Pools

If you're up for a bit of adventure and don't mind a moderately challenging hike, the Makapu'u Tide Pools are a hidden gem that promises an unforgettable experience. Located on Oahu's southeastern tip, these natural pools are formed by volcanic rock and are teeming with marine life. The journey begins with the Makapu'u Point Lighthouse Trail, a well-paved path that offers spectacular views of the coastline and the iconic lighthouse. About halfway up, a narrow, unofficial trail branches off towards the tide pools. The descent can be steep and rocky, so it's recommended for those with good physical fitness and proper footwear. Once you reach the tide pools, you'll be rewarded with crystal-clear water and the chance to see colorful fish, sea urchins, and other marine creatures up close. The pools are protected from the crashing waves, creating a calm environment perfect for snorkeling and swimming. However, it's essential to be mindful of the tide and surf conditions, as the area can be dangerous during high tide and rough seas.

Byodo-In Temple

Located at the foot of the Ko'olau Mountains in the Valley of the Temples Memorial Park, the Byodo-In Temple is a serene and spiritual retreat that offers a taste of Japan in the heart of Hawaii. This hidden gem is a smaller-scale replica of the over 950-year-old Byodo-In Temple in Uji, Japan, and was established in 1968 to commemorate the centennial of the first Japanese immigrants to Hawaii. The temple's grounds are stunning, featuring beautifully manicured Japanese gardens, koi ponds, and a large reflecting pond. The tranquility of the setting is enhanced by the sound of the large, three-ton brass bell, which visitors are invited to ring before entering the temple. The bell's deep tones are believed to purify the mind and bring good luck. Inside the temple, a serene golden Buddha statue sits as a symbol of peace and contemplation. The Byodo-In Temple is non-denominational and welcomes people of all faiths to enjoy its beauty and serenity. Walking through the gardens, feeding the koi fish, and meditating by the pond provide a deeply peaceful experience that contrasts with the more tourist-centric areas of Oahu.

4.4 Exploring Oahu's Neighborhoods

Oahu is an island of contrasts and harmonies, where vibrant urban centers meet serene beaches, and rich cultural history blends with modern charm. Exploring its neighborhoods reveals the true essence of this Hawaiian paradise, each area offering a unique slice of island life that will capture your heart and soul. From the bustling streets of Waikiki to the laid-back vibes of Kailua, the artistic soul of Kaka'ako, the historic charm of Chinatown, and the rustic allure of Haleiwa, Oahu's neighborhoods are a tapestry of experiences waiting to be discovered.

Waikiki

Waikiki is the heartbeat of Oahu, a neighborhood where the energy is palpable, and the allure is undeniable. Famous for its iconic beach, Waikiki is a vibrant blend of luxury, culture, and entertainment. Nestled along the southern shore of Honolulu, this neighborhood is easily accessible from any part of the island. Walking down Kalakaua Avenue, you'll be captivated by the mix of high-end boutiques, local shops, and world-class restaurants. The beach itself is a haven for sun-seekers and water sports enthusiasts, offering perfect waves for surfing and calm waters for swimming. As the sun sets, Waikiki's nightlife comes alive with beachfront bars, live music, and traditional luaus that offer a taste of Hawaiian culture. For a deeper dive into the area's history, visit the Waikiki Historic Trail, marked by bronze surfboard markers that tell the stories of Waikiki's past. The Royal Hawaiian Center and International Market Place provide a blend of shopping, dining, and cultural experiences, including hula shows and ukulele lessons. Waikiki is a place where every corner pulses with life, making it a must-visit for any traveler.

Kailua

In contrast to the bustling energy of Waikiki, Kailua on Oahu's windward coast offers a serene escape with its picturesque beaches and small-town charm. Just a 30-minute drive from Honolulu, Kailua is a haven for those seeking tranquility and natural beauty. Kailua Beach Park, with its powdery white sand and turquoise waters, is perfect for kayaking, paddleboarding, and simply relaxing under the Hawaiian sun. Nearby Lanikai Beach, often ranked among the world's best, provides a more secluded experience with stunning views of the Mokulua Islands. Kailua's town center is dotted with quaint boutiques, artisanal shops, and cozy cafes. The weekly Kailua Farmers' Market is a local favorite, offering fresh produce, handmade crafts, and delicious food from local vendors. Outdoor enthusiasts will love the numerous hiking trails, including the popular Lanikai Pillbox Hike, which rewards hikers with breathtaking panoramic views. Kailua is also known for its strong community spirit and sustainability efforts. Many businesses here promote eco-friendly practices, and there's a palpable sense of pride in preserving the natural beauty of the area. It's a neighborhood that invites you to slow down, connect with nature, and enjoy the simple pleasures of island life.

Kaka'ako

Kaka'ako, a former industrial district turned urban oasis, is the creative heart of Honolulu. Located between downtown Honolulu and Waikiki, this neighborhood has undergone a vibrant transformation, becoming a hub for artists, innovators, and entrepreneurs. Kaka'ako is renowned for its colorful street art, with murals painted by artists from around the world. A stroll through the streets feels like wandering through an open-air gallery, where every wall tells a story. The annual POW! WOW! Hawaii festival brings even more artistic energy to the area, with new murals and art installations popping up each year. The SALT at Our Kaka'ako complex is the neighborhood's centerpiece, offering a curated mix of local shops, eateries, and cultural spaces. Here, you can savor gourmet food, discover unique boutiques, and attend events ranging from yoga classes to live music performances. Kaka'ako Waterfront Park provides a green space where you can relax and enjoy the ocean views. Kaka'ako is also a culinary hotspot, home to some of Honolulu's trendiest restaurants and bars. Whether you're craving fresh poke, artisanal coffee, or craft cocktails, Kaka'ako's diverse dining scene has something to satisfy every palate. This neighborhood is a testament to Oahu's dynamic spirit, where innovation and tradition coexist harmoniously.

Chinatown

Steeped in history and rich with cultural diversity, Chinatown in downtown Honolulu is a neighborhood that tantalizes the senses. One of the oldest Chinatowns in the United States, this area is a vibrant mosaic of sights, sounds, and flavors. Chinatown's bustling streets are lined with traditional herbal shops, open-air markets, and historic buildings that transport you back in time. The Maunakea Marketplace is the heart of Chinatown, where you can find fresh produce, exotic spices, and unique trinkets. The neighborhood's culinary scene is a delightful blend of Chinese, Vietnamese, Filipino, and Hawaiian influences, offering everything from dim sum to pho. Cultural landmarks such as the Izumo Taishakyo Mission of Hawaii and the Hawaii Theatre Center add to the neighborhood's allure. The latter, known as the "Pride of the Pacific," hosts a variety of performances, from Broadway shows to local productions, reflecting the area's rich artistic heritage. Chinatown is also home to a burgeoning arts scene, with numerous galleries and studios showcasing the work of local artists. The First Friday Art Walk is a monthly event that draws art lovers to the area, transforming the streets into a lively celebration of creativity.

Exploring Chinatown is a sensory adventure, where every turn reveals a new discovery. It's a place where history and modernity blend seamlessly, creating a unique and dynamic neighborhood that's full of surprises.

Haleiwa

On the North Shore of Oahu, the charming town of Haleiwa offers a rustic escape that captures the essence of old Hawaii. Known as the gateway to the North Shore, Haleiwa is about an hour's drive from Honolulu, yet it feels like a world apart. Haleiwa's laid-back vibe and historic charm make it a perfect spot to unwind and soak in the island's natural beauty. The town's main street is lined with surf shops, art galleries, and eateries that reflect its surf culture and artistic spirit. Matsumoto Shave Ice, a local institution, is a must-visit for a refreshing treat after a day of exploring. The North Shore is famous for its world-class surf breaks, and Haleiwa is the ideal base for exploring beaches like Waimea Bay, Sunset Beach, and the Banzai Pipeline. These beaches offer some of the best surfing in the world, especially during the winter months when the waves are at their peak. Even if you're not a surfer, watching the pros tackle these massive waves is an exhilarating experience. For a more relaxed adventure, visit the Laniakea Beach, known for its resident sea turtles. A short hike from Haleiwa leads to the Waimea Valley, where you can explore botanical gardens and swim in a waterfall-fed pool.

4.5 Dining and Nightlife in Oahu

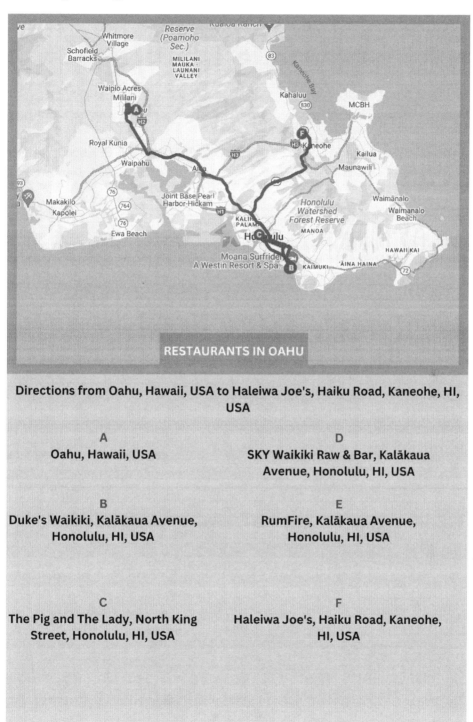

Directions from Oahu, Hawaii, USA to Haleiwa Joe's, Haiku Road, Kaneohe, HI, USA

A
Oahu, Hawaii, USA

B
Duke's Waikiki, Kalākaua Avenue, Honolulu, HI, USA

C
The Pig and The Lady, North King Street, Honolulu, HI, USA

D
SKY Waikiki Raw & Bar, Kalākaua Avenue, Honolulu, HI, USA

E
RumFire, Kalākaua Avenue, Honolulu, HI, USA

F
Haleiwa Joe's, Haiku Road, Kaneohe, HI, USA

Oahu, the beating heart of Hawaii, offers a culinary landscape as diverse and vibrant as its stunning scenery. The island's dining and nightlife scenes are a rich tapestry woven from traditional Hawaiian fare, international cuisine, and innovative culinary artistry. Whether you're seeking a romantic dinner by the sea, a bustling night out with friends, or a quiet cocktail in a hidden bar, Oahu delivers unforgettable experiences. Here are must-visit locations that encapsulate the best of Oahu's dining and nightlife.

Duke's Waikiki

Located on the iconic Waikiki Beach, Duke's Waikiki is more than just a restaurant; it's a celebration of Hawaiian culture and a tribute to the legendary Duke Kahanamoku, the father of modern surfing. The ambiance here is quintessentially Hawaiian, with open-air seating that offers stunning views of the Pacific Ocean, making it an ideal spot for both sunset dinners and late-night gatherings. Duke's menu is a delightful fusion of local flavors and classic American cuisine. Seafood lovers can indulge in fresh catches like macadamia nut-crusted mahi-mahi or coconut shrimp, while meat enthusiasts might savor a perfectly grilled rib-eye steak. Their famous Hula Pie, a towering concoction of ice cream, fudge, and macadamia nuts, is a must-try. Prices range from $15 for appetizers to $40 for main courses, making it accessible for a range of budgets. Duke's also features a vibrant bar scene, with tropical cocktails such as the Mai Tai and the Lava Flow being perennial favorites. Live music adds to the lively atmosphere, with local bands playing everything from traditional Hawaiian tunes to contemporary hits. Duke's is open from 7:00 AM to 11:00 PM, making it a perfect spot for breakfast, lunch, dinner, or late-night drinks.

The Pig & The Lady

In the heart of Chinatown, The Pig & The Lady stands out as a culinary gem, offering a unique blend of Vietnamese-inspired dishes with a modern twist. This family-run restaurant has garnered a loyal following for its inventive cuisine and warm, welcoming atmosphere. The industrial-chic décor, with its exposed brick walls and communal tables, adds to the trendy vibe. The Pig & The Lady's menu changes seasonally, reflecting the freshest local ingredients. Signature dishes include the Pho French Dip, a creative take on the classic Vietnamese soup, and the Laotian Fried Chicken, a flavorful fusion of spices and textures. Vegetarian options are plentiful and equally delightful. Prices here are mid-range, with appetizers around $10 and main dishes ranging from $15 to $25.

The restaurant also boasts an impressive cocktail menu, featuring handcrafted drinks that incorporate Asian flavors and Hawaiian spirits. The Lychee Martini and the Lemongrass Mojito are popular choices. The Pig & The Lady is open for lunch from 11:00 AM to 2:00 PM and for dinner from 5:30 PM to 9:00 PM, making it a great spot for a midday meal or an evening out.

Sky Waikiki

For those looking to dine with a view, Sky Waikiki offers an unparalleled experience. Located on the 19th floor of the Waikiki Business Plaza, this rooftop bar and restaurant provides breathtaking panoramic views of Waikiki Beach and the Honolulu skyline. The chic, modern décor and open-air setting create an elegant atmosphere perfect for both romantic dinners and lively nights out. Sky Waikiki's menu features a mix of contemporary American cuisine and Hawaiian influences. The seafood tower, loaded with fresh oysters, shrimp, and lobster, is a highlight, as are the Ahi Poke Tacos, which offer a delectable fusion of flavors. Entree prices range from $20 to $50, reflecting the upscale nature of the venue. The cocktail program at Sky Waikiki is equally impressive, with mixologists crafting innovative drinks that look as stunning as they taste. The signature Sky Tai, a tropical twist on the classic Mai Tai, and the Waikiki Sour, made with local spirits and fresh fruit, are must-tries. Sky Waikiki is open from

4:00 PM to midnight, offering a perfect transition from sunset cocktails to late-night revelry.

RumFire

Situated at the Sheraton Waikiki, RumFire is a beachfront bar and restaurant that offers an exciting fusion of Pacific Rim cuisine and vibrant nightlife. With its sleek, contemporary design and prime location, RumFire provides a dynamic setting for both dining and dancing under the stars. The menu at RumFire is designed for sharing, featuring small plates and tapas-style dishes that highlight local ingredients and bold flavors. Favorites include the Kalua Pork Nachos, Spicy Tuna Roll, and Hawaiian Poke Trio. Prices are reasonable, with most dishes ranging from $10 to $20, making it an ideal spot for groups looking to sample a variety of tastes. RumFire's extensive drink menu is centered around its impressive collection of rums from around the world, with over 100 varieties available. Signature cocktails such as the Mango Mojito and the Pineapple Express showcase the bar's creative approach to tropical mixology. Open from 11:00 AM to 2:00 AM, RumFire transitions seamlessly from a laid-back lunch spot to a bustling night-time destination, complete with live DJs and a dance floor.

Haleiwa Joe's

For a dining experience that captures the rustic charm of Oahu's North Shore, Haleiwa Joe's is a must-visit. Located in the historic town of Haleiwa, this restaurant offers a relaxed, island-style atmosphere with stunning views of the surrounding gardens and mountains. The open-air dining area, surrounded by lush greenery, creates a tranquil setting perfect for a leisurely meal. Haleiwa Joe's menu features a range of Pacific-inspired dishes, with a strong emphasis on fresh seafood and locally sourced ingredients. Highlights include the Prime Rib, a house specialty, and the Fresh Island Fish, prepared with tropical fruit salsa and a side of coconut rice. Prices are moderate, with appetizers around $12 and entrees between $20 and $35. The restaurant's bar serves a variety of tropical cocktails, local beers, and an extensive wine list. The Mai Tai and the Lava Flow are popular choices, perfectly complementing the flavorful dishes. Haleiwa Joe's is open from 4:30 PM to 9:00 PM for dinner, and from 11:00 AM to 2:00 PM on weekends for brunch, offering a serene dining experience that reflects the laid-back North Shore vibe.

CHAPTER 5
DISCOVERING MAUI

5.1 Overview of Maui

Step onto the shores of Maui, and you step into a world where the whispers of the past dance with the melodies of the present. This vibrant island, cradled in the embrace of the Pacific Ocean, holds within its embrace a tapestry woven with tales of ancient voyagers, fiery eruptions, and the resilient spirit of its people. Let me take you on a journey through time, back to the very genesis of this enchanting paradise. Picture the Polynesian navigators, courageous souls guided only by the stars and the wisdom passed down through generations. With their sturdy canoes slicing through the azure waves, they discovered the verdant beauty of Maui, a gem shimmering amidst the vastness of the ocean. It was a land rich in resources, where lush valleys kissed by gentle rains provided sustenance, and majestic mountains whispered secrets to those who dared to listen.

As centuries unfurled like delicate petals, Maui became a beacon of cultural richness and resilience. The echoes of chants and hula reverberated through its valleys, each movement a testament to the deep connection between the people and the land. Yet, Maui was not untouched by the tumultuous tides of history. With the arrival of European explorers came great change, bringing both prosperity and adversity to the island's shores. But through it all, Maui endured, its spirit unyielding like the molten heart of Haleakalā, the sacred volcano that watches over the land. Its landscapes, ever-changing yet timeless, offer a sanctuary for the weary soul and a playground for the adventurous spirit. From the lush rainforests of Hana to the golden sands of Ka'anapali, each corner of Maui beckons with a promise of discovery and wonder.

Today, as you walk beneath the swaying palms and feel the warmth of the sun upon your skin, you can't help but sense the whispers of those who came before. Their stories are etched into the very fabric of Maui, waiting to be uncovered by those who dare to listen. So, come, let Maui cast its spell upon you, and lose yourself in the magic of this captivating island. For in Maui, the past and present converge in a symphony of beauty and grace, inviting you to become a part of its timeless tale.

5.2 Must-See Attractions

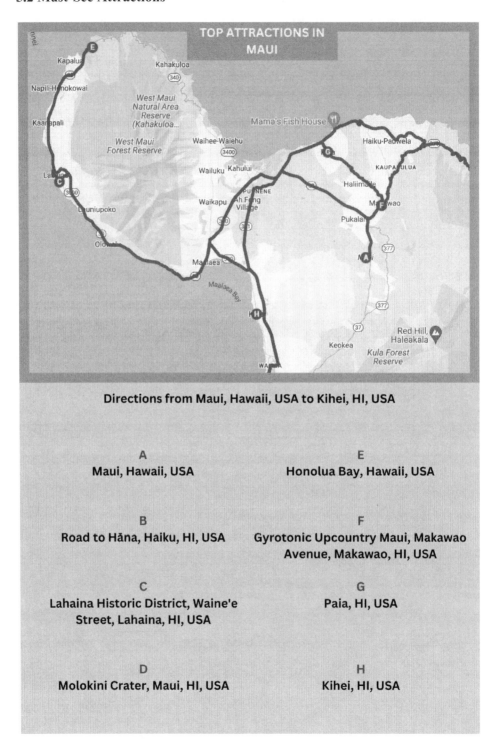

Directions from Maui, Hawaii, USA to Kihei, HI, USA

A
Maui, Hawaii, USA

B
Road to Hăna, Haiku, HI, USA

C
Lahaina Historic District, Waine'e Street, Lahaina, HI, USA

D
Molokini Crater, Maui, HI, USA

E
Honolua Bay, Hawaii, USA

F
Gyrotonic Upcountry Maui, Makawao Avenue, Makawao, HI, USA

G
Paia, HI, USA

H
Kihei, HI, USA

Welcome to Maui, a land where the whispers of the past mingle with the melodies of the present, and where every corner holds a story waiting to be told. As you embark on a journey through this enchanting paradise, prepare to be captivated by its diverse landscapes, rich history, and vibrant culture. From the rugged coastline of the Road to Hana to the ethereal beauty of Haleakalā National Park, Maui beckons with an array of must-see attractions that promise to leave you spellbound.

Each destination on this island holds its own unique allure, offering travelers a glimpse into the heart and soul of Maui. Whether you're seeking adventure, tranquility, or a deeper connection with nature, there's something here for everyone. So, join me as we embark on a voyage of discovery, uncovering the hidden gems that make Maui a destination like no other. Get ready to be inspired, enchanted, and utterly mesmerized by the beauty that awaits around every bend. Welcome to Maui, where every moment is an adventure waiting to unfold.

- 5.2.1 Road to Hana

Venturing along the iconic Road to Hana is akin to embarking on a journey through paradise itself. Located on the eastern side of Maui, this winding coastal road stretches approximately 64 miles, weaving its way through lush rainforests, cascading waterfalls, and dramatic cliffs that plunge into the sparkling waters of the Pacific Ocean. To embark on this unforgettable adventure, visitors can start their journey from Kahului or Paia and meander along the Hana Highway, taking in the breathtaking scenery along the way. While there is no official entry fee, it's essential to ensure your vehicle is in good condition, as the road is narrow and winding.

The Road to Hana isn't just a scenic drive; it's a portal to the heart and soul of Maui. Along the route, travelers can immerse themselves in the island's rich natural beauty, stopping at must-see attractions such as the enchanting Twin Falls, the serene Garden of Eden Arboretum, and the captivating Wailua Overlook. But it's not just about the destinations; it's about the journey itself. Each hairpin turn reveals a new vista, each waterfall whispers a tale of ancient legends, and each roadside fruit stand offers a taste of Maui's bounty. Whether you're hiking to hidden waterfalls, swimming in freshwater pools, or simply soaking in the panoramic views, the Road to Hana promises an unforgettable experience that will leave you spellbound.

- 5.2.2 Haleakalā National Park

Perched atop the summit of Maui's highest peak, Haleakalā National Park beckons travelers to witness the awe-inspiring beauty of its otherworldly landscapes. Spanning over 33,000 acres, this sacred wilderness is home to the world's largest dormant volcano, Haleakalā, whose name translates to "House of the Sun" in Hawaiian folklore. To reach this ethereal sanctuary, visitors can embark on a scenic drive up the winding Haleakalā Highway, which begins in the charming town of Kula. While there is an entry fee for vehicles entering the park, the experience is worth every penny.

Stepping into Haleakalā National Park is like stepping onto another planet. The lunar-like terrain, sculpted by centuries of volcanic activity, stretches as far as the eye can see, bathed in the soft glow of the rising sun. As dawn breaks over the horizon, visitors are treated to a mesmerizing sunrise that paints the sky in hues of orange and pink, a sight that has inspired poets and dreamers for generations. But the magic of Haleakalā extends far beyond its celestial vistas. Hiking enthusiasts can explore a network of trails that wind through lush forests, past ancient lava flows, and into the depths of majestic crater valleys.

Birdwatchers will delight in spotting rare species such as the endangered Hawaiian petrel, while cultural enthusiasts can learn about the rich history and traditions of the island's native people at the park's visitor centers.

- 5.2.3 Lahaina Historic District

Situated on the western coast of Maui lies the historic town of Lahaina, a charming seaside enclave steeped in the rich tapestry of Hawaii's past. Once a bustling whaling village and royal capital of the Hawaiian Kingdom, Lahaina has retained much of its old-world charm, with its quaint storefronts, historic landmarks, and vibrant cultural heritage. To immerse yourself in Lahaina's storied past, simply stroll along Front Street, the town's main thoroughfare, where you'll find an array of shops, galleries, and restaurants housed within meticulously preserved 19th-century buildings. While there is no entry fee to explore Lahaina, visitors may choose to embark on guided walking tours or visit the Baldwin Home Museum for a deeper insight into the town's history.

Lahaina's allure lies not only in its picturesque streets but also in its cultural significance. It was here that the legendary King Kamehameha I established his royal court, and where sailors from around the world once converged in search of fortune and adventure. Today, Lahaina pays homage to its heritage through annual festivals, traditional luaus, and the iconic Banyan Tree, a symbol of unity and resilience for the local community. From sampling fresh seafood at waterfront restaurants to browsing local art galleries and soaking in the sunset from Lahaina Harbor, there's no shortage of things to see and do in this timeless town. Whether you're a history buff, a culture enthusiast, or simply seeking a taste of authentic Hawaiian hospitality, Lahaina offers a glimpse into a bygone era that will leave you enchanted.

- 5.2.4 Molokini Crater

Tucked away in the cobalt waters of the Alalakeiki Channel, off the southwestern coast of Maui, lies a natural wonder unlike any other: Molokini Crater. This crescent-shaped islet, formed by the remnants of an ancient volcanic eruption, is renowned as one of the top snorkeling and diving destinations in the world. Reaching Molokini Crater is a breeze for visitors staying in popular resort areas such as Wailea or Kihei, as numerous boat tours depart daily from nearby harbors. While there is typically a fee to join a guided snorkeling excursion to Molokini, the experience of swimming alongside vibrant coral reefs and an abundance of marine life is priceless.

Beneath the surface of the crystalline waters surrounding Molokini, a kaleidoscope of colors awaits. Snorkelers and divers can marvel at schools of tropical fish darting through coral gardens, encounter graceful manta rays gliding effortlessly through the depths, and perhaps even catch a glimpse of the elusive monk seal or green sea turtle. But Molokini's appeal extends beyond its aquatic wonders. The crater itself is a designated marine sanctuary, teeming with biodiversity and ecological significance. It serves as a vital breeding ground for seabirds such as the wedge-tailed shearwater and the great frigatebird, making it a hotspot for birdwatchers and nature enthusiasts alike.

5.3 Hidden Gems of Maui

As you journey through the island's verdant landscapes and rugged coastlines, prepare to be enchanted by the secrets that lie just beyond the horizon. Beyond the well-trodden paths and tourist hotspots, Maui reveals itself as a tapestry of hidden gems, each one more captivating than the last. Join me on an odyssey of discovery as we unveil Maui's most cherished secrets, from secluded bays and mist-shrouded waterfalls to quaint towns steeped in history and culture. It's time to venture off the beaten path and immerse ourselves in the true essence of Maui, where every moment promises a new adventure and every corner holds a hidden treasure waiting to be uncovered. Welcome to Maui, where the journey is as enchanting as the destination itself.

Exploring Honolua Bay

Prepare to venture off the beaten path and discover the secluded paradise of Honolua Bay, nestled along Maui's northwestern coast. Here, hidden from the hustle and bustle of tourist crowds, lies a pristine sanctuary where vibrant coral reefs and crystal-clear waters beckon intrepid travelers. Snorkel amidst colorful marine life, ride the waves on some of the island's best surfing spots, and bask in the tranquility of this hidden gem.

Embracing Upcountry Maui

Embark on a journey into the heartland of Maui's Upcountry, where rolling hills and panoramic vistas await. Explore the charming town of Makawao, with its historic storefronts and Paniolo heritage, or lose yourself in the fragrant eucalyptus forests that carpet the countryside. Whether you're browsing local boutiques, savoring farm-to-table cuisine, or embarking on a scenic horseback ride, Upcountry Maui offers a glimpse into the island's timeless beauty and rich cultural heritage.

Chasing Waterfalls: Embark on a quest to discover Maui's mystical waterfalls, where the veil between the earthly realm and the ethereal realm grows thin. Journey deep into the heart of the rainforest to uncover hidden treasures such as the towering Waimoku Falls or the enchanting Seven Sacred Pools of Ohe'o. Feel the cool mist on your skin as you stand in awe of nature's majesty, and let the soothing sound of cascading waterfalls wash away your cares.

5.4 Exploring Maui's Towns

Maui, with its breathtaking natural beauty and vibrant cultural heritage, offers a tapestry of towns and villages waiting to be explored. From the historic charm of Lahaina to the laid-back vibe of Paia, each town beckons with its own unique allure, promising unforgettable experiences and cherished memories.

Paia: Paia, a haven for artists, surfers, and free spirits alike. Here, amidst the swaying coconut palms and colorful storefronts, you'll find a vibrant community that celebrates creativity, sustainability, and the aloha spirit. Explore Paia's quirky boutiques and art galleries, where local artisans showcase their talents through handmade jewelry, surf-inspired clothing, and eclectic works of art. Savor farm-to-table cuisine at trendy cafes and restaurants, where fresh, organic ingredients take center stage, or sample exotic flavors at the town's bustling food trucks and roadside stands.

Makawao: Escape the hustle and bustle of the coast and journey into the heart of Upcountry Maui, where the charming town of Makawao awaits. Known as the

"Cowboy Capital of Maui," Makawao exudes a rustic charm and old-world allure that harkens back to its days as a bustling ranching community. Stroll down Baldwin Avenue, where historic storefronts and art galleries offer a glimpse into Makawao's storied past and vibrant arts scene. Discover local treasures at the weekly farmers' market, where fresh produce, homemade crafts, and live music create a lively atmosphere that's quintessentially Maui. But Makawao isn't just for cowboys and artists; it's a town where outdoor enthusiasts can indulge in a variety of activities, from horseback riding and hiking to zip-lining and mountain biking.

Hana: Embark on a journey of discovery as you travel along the legendary Road to Hana to reach the idyllic town of Hana, a hidden gem nestled along Maui's eastern coast. Here, amidst the lush rainforests and cascading waterfalls, time seems to stand still, allowing visitors to immerse themselves in the serene beauty of nature. Explore Hana's pristine beaches, where golden sands meet turquoise waters and gentle waves beckon swimmers, snorkelers, and sunbathers alike. Visit iconic landmarks such as the Wai'anapanapa State Park, where dramatic sea caves, lava tubes, and black sand beaches await, or embark on a scenic hike through the verdant wilderness of the Haleakalā National Park.

Kihei: Experience the quintessential Hawaiian getaway in the sunny town of Kihei, where pristine beaches, vibrant nightlife, and endless sunshine await. Situated on Maui's southwestern coast, Kihei boasts some of the island's best weather year-round, making it the perfect destination for sun seekers and beach lovers alike. Spend your days soaking up the sun on Kihei's golden shores, where gentle waves lap against the shore and palm trees sway in the breeze. Snorkel amidst colorful coral reefs teeming with marine life, or try your hand at stand-up paddleboarding, kayaking, or windsurfing in the warm, crystal-clear waters of the Pacific Ocean.

5.5 Dining and Nightlife in Maui

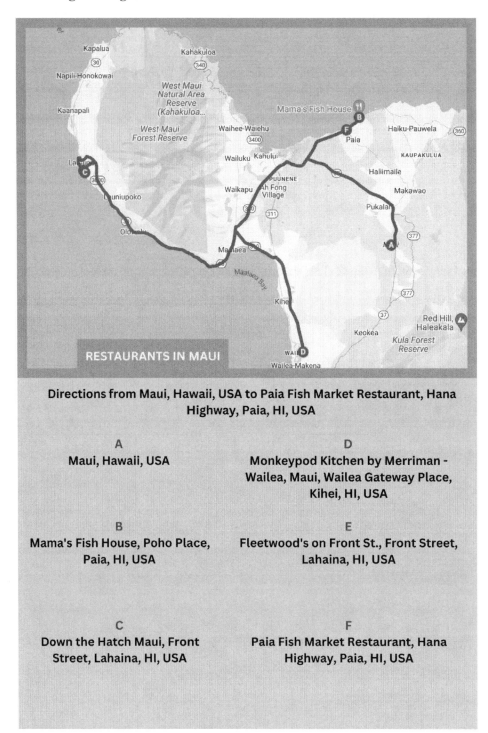

Directions from Maui, Hawaii, USA to Paia Fish Market Restaurant, Hana Highway, Paia, HI, USA

A
Maui, Hawaii, USA

D
Monkeypod Kitchen by Merriman - Wailea, Maui, Wailea Gateway Place, Kihei, HI, USA

B
Mama's Fish House, Poho Place, Paia, HI, USA

E
Fleetwood's on Front St., Front Street, Lahaina, HI, USA

C
Down the Hatch Maui, Front Street, Lahaina, HI, USA

F
Paia Fish Market Restaurant, Hana Highway, Paia, HI, USA

Maui is not just a destination for sun and surf; it's a haven for food lovers, where a diverse array of dining options and nightlife experiences beckon with promises of unforgettable flavors and unforgettable memories. From oceanfront fine dining to casual beachside eateries, each location offers its own unique blend of flavors, and ambiance. Join me on a journey of culinary discovery as we explore Maui's most beloved dining and nightlife destinations. From Lahaina's historic charm to Paia's bohemian vibe, each town holds its own culinary treasures waiting to be savored.

Mama's Fish House

Mama's Fish House is a culinary institution beloved by locals and visitors alike. This iconic restaurant boasts a breathtaking oceanfront setting, where diners can savor fresh seafood while enjoying panoramic views of the Pacific Ocean. At Mama's Fish House, the menu is a celebration of the island's bounty, with dishes crafted using locally sourced ingredients and traditional Hawaiian flavors. Indulge in specialties such as the Stuffed Mahi Mahi with lobster and crab, or the Polynesian Black Pearl dessert, a decadent chocolate mousse served in a tropical fruit shell. Mama's Fish House is open for lunch and dinner, with lunch hours from 11:00 AM to 3:00 PM and dinner service starting at 4:00 PM.

Lahaina Grill

Located in the heart of Lahaina's historic district, Lahaina Grill is a culinary gem known for its award-winning cuisine and elegant ambiance. Housed within a beautifully restored 19th-century building, this upscale restaurant offers a sophisticated dining experience that's perfect for a romantic evening out or a special celebration. The menu at Lahaina Grill showcases a fusion of global flavors with a focus on fresh, locally sourced ingredients. Start your meal with the famous Ahi Poke Tacos or the Lobster and Mango Salad, followed by entrees such as the Macadamia Nut Crusted Mahi Mahi or the Grilled Rack of Lamb. Lahaina Grill is open for dinner only, with service starting at 5:00 PM daily. Whether you're seeking a romantic dinner for two or an unforgettable dining experience with friends and family, Lahaina Grill promises an evening of culinary excellence and timeless elegance.

Monkeypod Kitchen by Merriman
Situated in the heart of Wailea's shopping and dining district, Monkeypod Kitchen by Merriman is a lively gastropub known for its inventive cocktails, creative cuisine, and vibrant atmosphere. With its open-air design and relaxed ambiance, this popular restaurant is the perfect spot for a casual meal or drinks with friends. The menu at Monkeypod Kitchen features a diverse selection of dishes inspired by Hawaiian flavors and global influences. Savor classics like the Kiawe Wood Oven Pizza or the Pan-Roasted Chicken, paired with signature cocktails crafted using fresh, locally sourced ingredients. Happy hour specials are available daily from 3:00 PM to 5:30 PM, offering discounted drinks and appetizers for those looking to enjoy a great meal without breaking the bank. Monkeypod Kitchen is open for lunch and dinner, with service starting at 11:00 AM daily. Whether you're craving innovative cuisine, craft cocktails, or simply a fun atmosphere to unwind, Monkeypod Kitchen promises an unforgettable dining experience that's sure to leave you coming back for more.

Fleetwood's on Front St.
Perched atop Lahaina's bustling Front Street, Fleetwood's on Front St. is a vibrant dining and entertainment venue named after legendary musician Mick Fleetwood. This iconic restaurant offers a unique blend of live music, delicious cuisine, and stunning ocean views, making it a favorite destination for locals and visitors alike. The menu at Fleetwood's features a mix of classic American dishes and island-inspired fare, with highlights such as the Fleetwood's Seafood Tower, the Maui Cattle Company Burger, and the Fresh Catch of the Day. Pair your meal with a selection from the extensive wine list or enjoy a handcrafted

cocktail from the rooftop bar. Fleetwood's on Front St. is open for lunch and dinner, with service starting at 11:00 AM daily.

Paia Fish Market

Tucked away in the charming town of Paia on Maui's north shore, the Paia Fish Market is a beloved local institution known for its casual atmosphere and fresh, flavorful seafood. Housed within a laid-back storefront adorned with colorful murals and surf decor, this no-frills eatery offers a taste of authentic Hawaiian cuisine without the fuss. The menu at Paia Fish Market is simple yet satisfying, with a focus on locally caught seafood served up in generous portions. Choose from a variety of fish tacos, sandwiches, and plate lunches, or opt for the signature Fish Market Plate, which allows diners to create their own seafood combo. Paia Fish Market is open for lunch and dinner, with service starting at 11:00 AM daily.

CHAPTER 6
EXPLORING BIG ISLAND (HAWAII ISLAND)

6.1 Overview of Big Island

In the vast expanse of the Pacific Ocean lies a gem unlike any other, the Big Island of Hawaii. Its story begins millions of years ago, born from the fiery depths of the Earth itself. Picture this: molten lava erupting from beneath the ocean's surface, forming majestic mountains that rise proudly against the azure sky. This island, the youngest in the Hawaiian archipelago, is a testament to the raw power of nature and the resilience of life. But let's rewind the tape of time even further. Legend has it that Pele, the fiery goddess of volcanoes, made her home on these lands. Her presence is felt in every volcanic eruption, every lava flow that shapes the island's ever-changing landscape. The ancient Hawaiians revered her, offering prayers and sacrifices to appease her fiery temper. To this day, her spirit is said to dwell within the depths of Kilauea, one of the world's most active volcanoes.

As centuries passed, the island became a haven for Polynesian voyagers seeking new horizons. They arrived on double-hulled canoes, guided only by the stars and the whispers of the wind. These brave explorers brought with them not only their traditions and customs but also their deep connection to the land and sea. The arrival of Western explorers in the 18th century marked a new chapter in the island's history. They were mesmerized by the island's beauty, its lush valleys, pristine beaches, and vibrant coral reefs. But with their arrival came great change. Missionaries sought to convert the native Hawaiians to Christianity, while traders introduced new technologies and diseases that forever altered the island's way of life. Despite these challenges, the spirit of aloha endured. It is a spirit of love, compassion, and respect for all living things. It is reflected in the warmth of the Hawaiian people, their rich cultural traditions, and their deep connection to the land.

Today, the Big Island stands as a testament to the resilience of the human spirit and the power of nature to heal and inspire. Visitors from around the world come to marvel at its wonders, from the fiery lava flows of Kilauea to the snow-capped peaks of Mauna Kea. They immerse themselves in the island's rich tapestry of culture and history, savoring the taste of fresh poke, swaying to the rhythm of traditional hula, and basking in the warm embrace of aloha. But beyond its natural beauty and cultural heritage, the Big Island offers something even more precious: a sense of awe and wonder that transcends time and space. It is a place where dreams are born, where memories are made, and where the spirit of aloha lives on in every sunrise and sunset.

6.2 Must-See Attractions

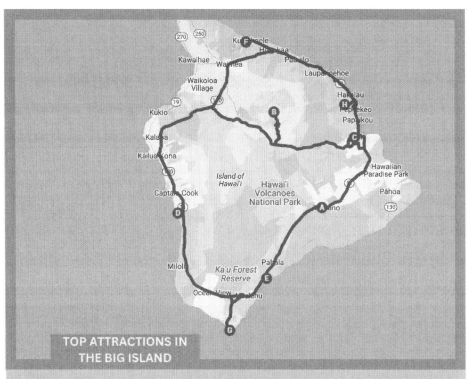

Directions from Hawaii Volcanoes National Park, HI, USA to 'Akaka Falls, Hawaii, USA

A
Hawaii Volcanoes National Park, HI, USA

B
Mauna Kea Observatory, Hawaii, USA

C
Rainbow Falls, Hilo, HI, USA

D
Pu'uhonua O Honaunau National Historical Park, State Highway 160, Hōnaunau, HI, USA

E
Punalu'u Black Sand Beach, Ninole Loop Road, Naalehu, HI, USA

F
Waipio Valley, Hawaii, USA

G
Papakōlea Green Sand Beach, Naalehu, HI, USA

H
Akaka Falls, Hawaii, USA

The Big Island of Hawaii is a land of contrasts, where ancient traditions meet modern innovation, and natural wonders abound at every turn. Our journey begins amidst the fiery landscapes of Hawaii Volcanoes National Park, where the earth's primal forces have sculpted a canvas of unparalleled beauty. Here, amidst the smoldering craters and steaming vents, we bear witness to the raw power of nature, where molten lava meets the sea in a dance as old as time itself. But our quest for discovery does not end there, for atop the towering summit of Mauna Kea Observatory, we turn our gaze skyward, seeking answers to the mysteries of the cosmos. Here, amidst the pristine darkness of the night sky, we are humbled by the vastness of the universe and the boundless possibilities that lie beyond. Descending from the heavens, we find ourselves in the quaint town of Hilo, where the rhythm of life beats to the tune of ancient traditions and modern innovation. Here, amidst the lush rainforests and cascading waterfalls, we immerse ourselves in the rich tapestry of Hawaiian culture, where every stone tells a story and every breeze carries the whispers of the past.

- 6.2.1 Hawaii Volcanoes National Park

Hawaii Volcanoes National Park stands as a testament to the island's fiery origins and ever-evolving landscape. This UNESCO World Heritage Site encompasses over 300,000 acres of dramatic volcanic terrain, including the iconic Kilauea and Mauna Loa volcanoes. To reach the park, visitors can embark on a scenic drive along the Chain of Craters Road, which winds through ancient lava fields, lush rainforests, and steaming volcanic vents. Admission to the park is $30 per vehicle or $15 per individual on foot, and the park is open 24 hours a day. A visit to Hawaii Volcanoes National Park offers a rare opportunity to witness the raw power of nature in action. Visitors can explore a network of hiking trails that lead to volcanic craters, lava tubes, and other geological wonders. Highlights include the mesmerizing glow of the Halema'uma'u Crater, the otherworldly landscapes of the Ka'u Desert, and the lush fern-filled forests of the Thurston Lava Tube.

- 6.2.2 Mauna Kea Observatory

Perched atop the tallest peak in the Pacific, Mauna Kea Observatory offers a window into the cosmos unlike any other. Located on the summit of Mauna Kea at an elevation of over 13,000 feet, this world-renowned astronomical observatory boasts some of the clearest and darkest skies on Earth. Getting to Mauna Kea Observatory requires a four-wheel-drive vehicle due to the steep and rugged terrain. While there is no entry fee to access the summit, visitors are encouraged to check in at the Onizuka Center for International Astronomy Visitor Information Station (VIS) located at the 9,200-foot level for safety information and to acclimate to the altitude. Once atop Mauna Kea, visitors are treated to panoramic views of the island below and the vast expanse of the night sky above. The observatory is home to a collection of cutting-edge telescopes operated by research institutions from around the world, offering visitors a chance to peer deep into the cosmos and unlock the mysteries of the universe.

- 6.2.3 Hilo and Rainbow Falls

Situated on the eastern coast of the Big Island, Hilo is a charming town steeped in history and surrounded by natural beauty. One of its most iconic attractions is Rainbow Falls, a breathtaking waterfall cascading over a natural lava cave into a tranquil pool below. Getting to Hilo is easy, with daily flights from Honolulu International Airport and a scenic drive along the Hamakua Coast. Rainbow Falls is located just a short drive from downtown Hilo, with ample parking available for visitors. There is no entry fee to access the falls, making it an affordable and accessible attraction for all. A visit to Rainbow Falls offers more than just a chance to marvel at its natural beauty. According to Hawaiian legend, the pool below the waterfall is inhabited by the mischievous mo'o, or lizard guardians, who protect the area from harm. Visitors can explore the surrounding trails and lush tropical gardens, or simply relax and soak in the serene atmosphere.

- 6.2.4 Pu'uhonua o Hōnaunau National Historical Park

Pu'uhonua o Hōnaunau National Historical Park is a sacred site steeped in Hawaiian tradition and lore. This ancient sanctuary served as a place of refuge for those who violated kapu, or sacred laws, offering them a chance at redemption and forgiveness. To reach Pu'uhonua o Hōnaunau National Historical Park, visitors can take a scenic drive along the Mamalahoa Highway, with ample parking available onsite. Admission to the park is $15 per vehicle or $7 per individual on foot, and the park is open daily from sunrise to sunset.

A visit to Pu'uhonua o Hōnaunau offers a glimpse into the spiritual and cultural practices of ancient Hawaii. Visitors can explore the grounds of the sanctuary, which include a reconstructed temple, royal fishponds, and sacred stone carvings. Interpretive exhibits and guided tours provide insights into the history and significance of the site, allowing visitors to connect with the traditions of the past. In addition to its cultural significance, Pu'uhonua o Hōnaunau is also a haven for wildlife, with pristine beaches, coral reefs, and crystal-clear waters teeming with marine life. Visitors can snorkel, swim, or simply relax and soak in the natural beauty of the area.

6.3 Hidden Gems of Big Island

As we embark on our journey to explore the enchanting Big Island of Hawaii, we are beckoned not only by its renowned attractions but also by the hidden gems that lie off the beaten path, waiting to be discovered by the intrepid traveler. These hidden treasures, shrouded in mystery and steeped in history, hold the key to unlocking the soul of this magical land.

Punalu'u Black Sand Beach

Along the southeastern coast of the Big Island lies a hidden gem unlike any other: Punalu'u Black Sand Beach. Here, amidst the rugged beauty of the coastline, the sands are as black as night, a testament to the island's volcanic origins. But it is not just the striking contrast of black sand against turquoise waters that draws visitors to this secluded paradise. Punalu'u is also home to a diverse array of wildlife, including endangered hawksbill and green sea turtles, which can often be spotted basking in the sun on the beach's pristine shores. A visit to Punalu'u Black Sand Beach is not just a journey through geological time but also a chance to connect with the fragile ecosystems that call this island home.

Waipi'o Valley

Hidden away on the northeastern coast of the Big Island lies Waipi'o Valley, a verdant oasis of lush rainforests, cascading waterfalls, and towering cliffs that plunge into the sea below. Accessible only by foot, horseback, or 4WD vehicle, this remote valley is steeped in Hawaiian history and mythology. According to legend, Waipi'o was once the residence of the Hawaiian gods and served as a place of refuge for ancient Hawaiian kings. Today, it offers visitors a chance to escape the hustle and bustle of modern life and immerse themselves in the tranquility of nature. Whether hiking to the valley floor, exploring hidden waterfalls, or simply taking in the breathtaking views from the overlook, a visit to Waipi'o Valley is sure to leave a lasting impression on the soul.

Papakōlea Green Sand Beach

Tucked away on the southern tip of the Big Island lies a hidden gem that defies imagination: Papakōlea Green Sand Beach. Accessible only by a rugged hike or 4WD vehicle, this secluded beach is renowned for its unique olive-green sands, a result of the presence of the mineral olivine. As we traverse the rocky coastline and descend upon the beach, we are greeted by a sight unlike any other, where the verdant hues of the sand blend seamlessly with the azure waters of the Pacific Ocean. But Papakōlea is more than just a natural wonder; it is also a sacred site revered by the native Hawaiians, who believe it to be the dwelling place of the goddess Pele. A visit to Papakōlea Green Sand Beach is not just a journey through geological time but also a chance to connect with the spiritual essence of the island.

Akaka Falls

Hidden amidst the lush rainforests of the Hamakua Coast lies a hidden treasure of immense beauty: Akaka Falls. Tumbling over 400 feet into a tranquil pool below, these majestic falls are a sight to behold, their misty veil creating rainbows that dance in the sunlight. As we wander along the well-maintained trails that wind through the surrounding jungle, we are enveloped in a symphony of sights and sounds, from the vibrant colors of tropical flowers to the melodic songs of native birds. But it is not just the natural beauty of Akaka Falls that captivates the soul; it is also the sense of peace and serenity that pervades the air, a reminder of the healing power of nature in our busy lives.

Puako Petroglyph Archaeological Preserve

Hidden away on the western coast of the Big Island lies a treasure trove of ancient artistry: the Puako Petroglyph Archaeological Preserve. Here, amidst the rugged lava fields that stretch towards the sea, we discover thousands of petroglyphs carved into the volcanic rock by the native Hawaiians over a thousand years ago. These mysterious symbols offer a glimpse into the rich cultural heritage of the island, telling stories of gods and goddesses, warriors and chiefs, and the everyday lives of the people who once called this land home. As we wander among the ancient stones, we are transported back in time, our imaginations ignited by the whispers of the past.

6.4 Exploring Big Island's Regions

As we set foot upon the sprawling landscapes of Big Island, we are greeted by a tapestry of diversity that beckons us to explore every corner, from the fiery depths of its volcanic heart to the lush greenery of its tropical rainforests. Join me on a journey through distinct regions of this majestic island, where adventure and wonder await at every turn.

The Volcanic Majesty of Kilauea and Puna: Our journey begins amidst the fiery landscapes of Kilauea and Puna, where the earth's primal forces shape the very fabric of the island. Here, amidst the smoldering craters and steaming vents of Hawaii Volcanoes National Park, we bear witness to the raw power of nature, where molten lava flows like rivers of fire and new land is born with each passing moment. As we traverse the otherworldly terrain, we are enveloped in a sense of awe and wonder, humbled by the immense forces at play beneath our feet.

The Serenity of Hamakua and Hilo: As we journey northward, we find ourselves immersed in the tranquil beauty of Hamakua and Hilo, where verdant valleys and cascading waterfalls paint a picture of serenity and peace. Here, amidst the lush rainforests and fertile farmlands, we discover hidden gems waiting to be uncovered by the intrepid traveler. From the majestic Akaka Falls to the picturesque town of Hilo, there is no shortage of wonders to behold in this region. But it is not just the natural beauty that captivates the soul; it is also the rich cultural heritage that permeates the air. In Hilo, we are greeted by the rhythmic beat of ancient hula dances and the melodic strains of traditional music. Here, amidst the bustling farmers' markets and historic landmarks, we find ourselves immersed in the vibrant tapestry of Hawaiian culture, where every corner tells a story and every moment is a celebration of life.

The Majesty of Mauna Kea and Waimea: As we journey inland, we find ourselves surrounded by the majestic beauty of Mauna Kea and Waimea, where snow-capped peaks and rolling hills paint a picture of timeless grandeur. Here, amidst the towering summits and vast expanses of grasslands, we discover a sense of peace and tranquility that can only be found in the embrace of nature. But it is not just the breathtaking vistas that captivate the soul; it is also the sense of adventure that beckons us to explore further. In Mauna Kea, we ascend to the summit of the tallest mountain in the Pacific, where the heavens stretch out before us in all their splendor. Here, amidst the celestial wonders of the universe, we find ourselves humbled by the vastness of space and the beauty of the cosmos.

The Serenity of Kohala and Kona: As we journey westward, we find ourselves immersed in the serene beauty of Kohala and Kona, where golden beaches and crystal-clear waters beckon us to relax and unwind. Here, amidst the swaying palms and gentle breezes, we discover a sense of peace and tranquility that soothes the soul. But it is not just the idyllic beaches that captivate the soul; it is also the rich cultural heritage that permeates the air. In Kona, we discover ancient Hawaiian temples and sacred sites, where the spirits of the past linger in the air. Here, amidst the vibrant colors and vibrant traditions, we find ourselves transported back in time to a world of ancient legends and timeless wonders.

The Untamed Beauty of Ka'u and South Point: As we journey southward, we find ourselves immersed in the untamed beauty of Ka'u and South Point, where rugged coastlines and windswept cliffs paint a picture of wild and untamed beauty. Here, amidst the crashing waves and jagged rocks, we discover a sense of adventure that calls to the soul. But it is not just the rugged landscapes that captivate the soul; it is also the sense of freedom that comes from exploring the unknown. In South Point, we discover the southernmost point of the United States, where the land meets the sea in a dramatic clash of elements.

6.5 Dining and Nightlife on Big Island

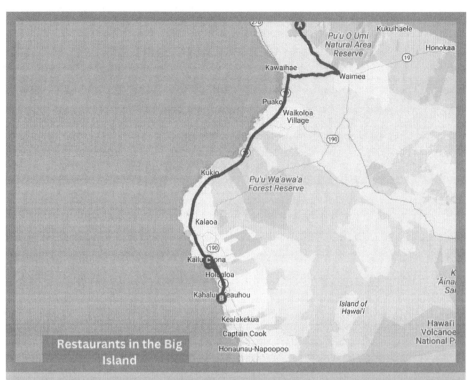

Restaurants in the Big Island

Directions from Paniolo BBQ Dinner, Waimea, HI, USA to Honu's on the Beach, Palani Road, Kailua- Kona, HI, USA

A
Paniolo BBQ Dinner, Waimea, HI, USA

B
Sea Paradise, Kaleiopapa Street, Kailua-Kona, HI, USA

C
Big Island Grill, Kuakini Highway, Kailua-Kona, HI, USA

D
On the Rocks, Kahakai Road, Kailua-Kona, HI, USA

E
Huggo's, Kahakai Road, Kailua-Kona, HI, USA

F
Honu's on the Beach, Palani Road, Kailua-Kona, HI, USA

The Big Island of Hawaii, known for its diverse landscapes ranging from volcanic deserts to lush rainforests, offers an equally diverse and captivating dining and nightlife scene. Whether you're seeking a rustic BBQ dinner under the stars, an oceanfront dining experience, or a vibrant night out with live music and tropical cocktails, the Big Island has something to satisfy every craving. Here, we delve into exceptional locations that showcase the island's rich culinary and entertainment offerings.

Paniolo BBQ Dinner

Set in the picturesque countryside of Waimea, the Paniolo BBQ Dinner is an immersive dining experience that captures the spirit of Hawaii's cowboy, or "paniolo," heritage. This event takes place at the Anna Ranch Heritage Center, a historic site that offers a glimpse into the island's ranching past. The atmosphere is rustic and welcoming, with communal picnic tables set under the open sky, surrounded by rolling green pastures and the majestic Kohala Mountains. The menu at the Paniolo BBQ Dinner is a hearty feast that highlights local ingredients and traditional BBQ fare. Guests can enjoy succulent grilled meats such as teriyaki-glazed ribs, Hawaiian-style pulled pork, and BBQ chicken, accompanied by sides like creamy coleslaw, corn on the cob, and baked beans. A selection of local craft beers and wines is available to complement the meal. Prices for this all-inclusive experience range from $60 to $80 per person, depending on the season and special events.

Sea Paradise

For a dining experience that combines gourmet cuisine with breathtaking ocean views, Sea Paradise in Kailua-Kona offers an unforgettable evening on the water. This unique venue provides a sunset dinner cruise aboard a luxurious catamaran, where guests can enjoy the stunning coastal scenery and the chance to spot marine life such as dolphins and whales. The menu on Sea Paradise features a selection of locally sourced dishes that highlight the flavors of the island. Appetizers include fresh poke and tropical fruit platters, while the main course options range from grilled mahi-mahi with a mango salsa to tender beef tenderloin with a Kona coffee rub. Vegetarian and gluten-free options are also available to cater to all dietary needs. Prices for the dinner cruise are around $120 to $150 per person, which includes the meal, beverages, and the cruise itself.

As the sun sets over the Pacific Ocean, the ambiance on board becomes magical. Guests can sip on tropical cocktails such as Mai Tais and Blue Hawaiians while enjoying the gentle ocean breeze and live music. The cruise departs from Keauhou Bay and lasts approximately three hours, running from 5:00 PM to 8:00 PM. Reservations are highly recommended, as this popular experience often sells out.

Big Island Grill

Located in the heart of Kailua-Kona, Big Island Grill is a beloved local eatery known for its generous portions and homestyle Hawaiian comfort food. This family-friendly restaurant offers a casual and inviting atmosphere, making it a perfect spot for breakfast, lunch, or dinner. The menu at Big Island Grill features a wide variety of dishes that cater to all tastes. Breakfast favorites include the Loco Moco, a classic Hawaiian dish with rice, hamburger patty, fried egg, and gravy, and the Macadamia Nut Pancakes served with coconut syrup. For lunch and dinner, options range from fresh seafood plates, such as ahi tuna and shrimp scampi, to hearty meat dishes like prime rib and kalua pork. Prices are reasonable, with most entrees priced between $10 and $20. Big Island Grill also offers a selection of refreshing beverages, including tropical smoothies, local beers, and house-made lemonades. The restaurant is open from 7:00 AM to 9:00 PM daily, making it a convenient choice for any meal. With its friendly service and consistently delicious food, Big Island Grill is a favorite among both locals and visitors.

On the Rocks

For those looking to enjoy a relaxed meal and drinks with their toes in the sand, On the Rocks in Kailua-Kona offers the quintessential beachside dining experience. Located right on the water's edge, this open-air restaurant and bar provide stunning views of Kailua Bay and a laid-back atmosphere perfect for unwinding after a day of exploring.

The menu at On the Rocks emphasizes fresh, local ingredients and includes a variety of seafood, burgers, salads, and pupus (appetizers). Highlights include the Grilled Fish Tacos, served with a tangy mango salsa, and the Ahi Poke Bowl, featuring fresh ahi tuna and seaweed salad over rice. Prices range from $12 for appetizers to $25 for main courses, offering good value for the quality and location. The bar at On the Rocks serves up an array of tropical cocktails, local beers, and wines. The signature drink, the "Lava Flow," is a refreshing blend of rum, coconut cream, and strawberry puree, perfect for sipping while watching the sunset. Live music is a staple here, with local musicians performing daily from 6:00 PM to 9:00 PM, enhancing the already vibrant atmosphere. On the Rocks is open from 11:00 AM to 10:00 PM, providing a seamless transition from lunch to dinner and beyond.

Huggo's

Huggo's, also located in Kailua-Kona, is an iconic oceanfront restaurant that has been a staple of the Big Island's dining scene since 1969. Known for its romantic setting and innovative cuisine, Huggo's offers an upscale yet relaxed dining experience that captures the essence of island living. The menu at Huggo's showcases a blend of traditional Hawaiian flavors and contemporary culinary techniques. Guests can start their meal with appetizers like Coconut Shrimp or the Huggo's Caesar Salad, followed by entrees such as Macadamia Nut-Crusted Mahimahi, Hawaiian-style Ribeye Steak, or the fresh catch of the day, prepared with a variety of tropical sauces. Prices are on the higher side, reflecting the restaurant's premium location and quality, with entrees ranging from $30 to $50. Huggo's also features an extensive wine list, along with signature cocktails like the "Huggos' Mai Tai" and the "Kona Hurricane." The restaurant's open-air seating allows diners to enjoy unobstructed views of the ocean, making it a perfect spot for a sunset dinner. Live music performances add to the enchanting atmosphere, with local artists playing Hawaiian and contemporary tunes nightly. Huggo's is open from 5:00 PM to 9:00 PM, and reservations are recommended, especially for those seeking a table with a view.

Honu's on the Beach

Honu's on the Beach, located at the Courtyard King Kamehameha's Kona Beach Hotel, offers a dining experience that combines fine cuisine with breathtaking ocean views. This beachfront restaurant in Kailua-Kona is known for its elegant setting and exceptional service. The menu at Honu's on the Beach features a blend of Hawaiian and international dishes. Guests can start with appetizers like Ahi Poke and Crab Cakes, followed by entrees such as Grilled Opakapaka, Herb-Crusted Rack of Lamb, and the Honu's Signature Seafood Platter. Vegetarian and vegan options are also available. Prices for entrees range from $25 to $50, reflecting the restaurant's upscale nature. The bar serves a wide selection of wines, craft cocktails, and local beers. Signature drinks include the "Honu's Mai Tai" and the "Island Breeze," both perfect for enjoying the sunset. Honu's on the Beach is open for breakfast, lunch, and dinner, from 6:30 AM to 9:00 PM, offering a versatile dining option for any time of day.

CHAPTER 7
DISCOVERING KAUAI

7.1 Overview of Kauai

Kauai, the oldest and most enchanting island in the Hawaiian archipelago. Its history whispers tales of ancient voyages, epic battles, and the resilient spirit of its people, echoing through lush valleys and towering cliffs, beckoning travelers to uncover its secrets. Legend has it that Kauai was birthed by the gods themselves, emerging from the depths of the ocean in a fiery display of creation. Its rugged coastline, adorned with cascading waterfalls and pristine beaches, bears witness to this divine touch, inviting visitors to explore its untamed wilderness. The history of Kauai is etched in the land, a story of courage and perseverance passed down through generations. Long before the arrival of Captain James Cook, the island was inhabited by the fearless Polynesians, who navigated the vast expanse of the Pacific Ocean guided only by the stars. Their voyages brought them to the shores of Kauai, where they forged a deep connection with the land, cultivating taro fields and fishing the abundant waters.

Centuries later, European explorers set sail for the distant shores of Hawaii, drawn by tales of paradise and adventure. Among them was Captain Cook, who stumbled upon Kauai in 1778 during his fateful voyage across the Pacific. His encounter with the island marked the beginning of a new chapter in its history, as waves of foreign influence swept ashore, forever shaping its culture and landscape. But amidst the winds of change, Kauai remained steadfast in its identity, preserving its traditions and customs against the tide of modernization. Today, remnants of its storied past can be found in every corner of the island, from ancient Hawaiian temples to quaint plantation towns, each bearing witness to the resilience of its people.

To experience Kauai is to embark on a journey through time, where the echoes of the past mingle with the beauty of the present. Whether hiking along the rugged Na Pali Coast, exploring the lush valleys of Waimea Canyon, or simply basking in the warmth of the sun on Poipu Beach, every moment spent on this island is a testament to its enduring legacy.

7.2 Must-See Attractions

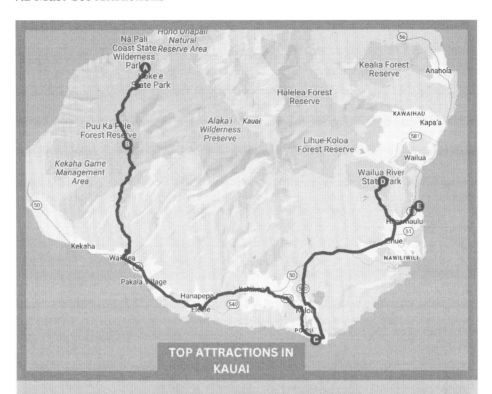

Directions from Nā Pali Coast State Wilderness Park, Hawaii, USA to Hawaiian Rainforest Spa, Kauai Beach Drive, Lihue, Kauai, HI, USA

A
Nā Pali Coast State Wilderness Park, Hawaii, USA

B
Waimea Canyon State Park, Waimea, HI, USA

D
Wailua Falls, Hawaii, USA

C
Poipu Beach Park, Hoone Road, Koloa, HI, USA

E
Hawaiian Rainforest Spa, Kauai Beach Drive, Lihue, Kauai, HI, USA

Kauai stands as a testament to the raw, unbridled beauty of nature. As the oldest and most captivating island in the Hawaiian archipelago, it beckons travelers from far and wide with promises of adventure, tranquility, and discovery. Within its lush valleys and along its rugged coastline, lie treasures waiting to be unearthed, each more enchanting than the last. From the towering cliffs of the Na Pali Coast to the majestic depths of Waimea Canyon, Kauai boasts an array of must-see attractions that capture the imagination and stir the soul. Join me on a journey through this island paradise as we explore five of its most iconic destinations, each offering a glimpse into the rich tapestry of history, culture, and natural wonder that defines Kauai. Embark on this adventure with an open heart and a spirit of curiosity, for in Kauai, every moment holds the promise of discovery and delight.

- 7.2.1 Na Pali Coast

Na Pali Coast, a rugged stretch of coastline renowned for its dramatic cliffs, lush valleys, and pristine beaches. Accessible only by foot, boat, or helicopter, this iconic landmark offers visitors a glimpse into the untouched beauty of Hawaii's natural landscape. To reach the Na Pali Coast by land, adventurous souls can embark on the Kalalau Trail, a challenging 11-mile hike that winds its way through verdant valleys and towering cliffs. Along the way, hikers are treated to panoramic views of the Pacific Ocean and the lush valleys below, making it a truly unforgettable experience.

For those seeking a more leisurely approach, boat tours and helicopter rides offer a bird's-eye view of the coastline, allowing visitors to marvel at the sheer magnitude of its beauty from above. Whether by land, sea, or air, a visit to the Na Pali Coast is sure to leave a lasting impression on all who venture there.

- ## 7.2.2 Waimea Canyon State Park

Dubbed the *"Grand Canyon of the Pacific,"* Waimea Canyon State Park is a geological wonder nestled in the heart of Kauai. Carved over millennia by the erosive forces of wind and water, this majestic canyon stretches for 14 miles and plunges to depths of over 3,000 feet, creating a stunning tapestry of colors and textures. Located on the island's west side, Waimea Canyon is easily accessible by car via Highway 550. Upon arrival, visitors are greeted by panoramic viewpoints that offer sweeping vistas of the canyon below, each more breathtaking than the last. For the more adventurous, hiking trails meander through the park, providing opportunities to explore its hidden waterfalls and lush forests. With its awe-inspiring beauty and rich geological history, Waimea Canyon State Park is a must-see attraction for anyone visiting Kauai. Whether marveling at its sheer magnitude from above or trekking through its rugged terrain, the canyon's beauty is sure to leave a lasting impression on all who behold it.

- ## 7.2.3 Poipu Beach Park

Situated on Kauai's sunny south shore, Poipu Beach Park is a picturesque paradise renowned for its pristine sands, crystal-clear waters, and abundant marine life. Named one of America's best beaches, this idyllic stretch of coastline offers something for everyone, from sunbathing and swimming to snorkeling and surfing. Access to Poipu Beach Park is easy, with ample parking and facilities available for visitors. Once there, beachgoers can relax on the golden sands, take a dip in the calm waters, or explore the vibrant coral reefs teeming with colorful fish and sea turtles. For those seeking adventure, nearby attractions such as Spouting Horn and Allerton Garden offer opportunities to explore Kauai's natural beauty further. Whether relaxing on the beach or exploring the surrounding area, a visit to Poipu Beach Park is sure to be a highlight of any trip to Kauai.

- **7.2.4 Wailua Falls**

Tucked away in the lush heart of Kauai lies Wailua Falls, a majestic cascade that plunges 80 feet into a tranquil pool below. Named after the Wailua River that feeds it, this iconic waterfall is steeped in both natural beauty and cultural significance, making it a must-see attraction for visitors to the island. Located just off the main highway in eastern Kauai, Wailua Falls is easily accessible by car, with parking available nearby. From there, visitors can enjoy panoramic views of the waterfall from a lookout point above or venture down to the base for a closer look. In addition to its stunning natural beauty, Wailua Falls holds a special place in Hawaiian folklore and history. According to legend, it was here that the ancient Hawaiian chiefs would test the courage of their warriors by leaping from the top of the falls into the pool below, a tradition known as "lele kawa." Today, visitors can pay homage to this rich cultural heritage while marveling at the beauty of Wailua Falls, making it a truly unforgettable experience for all who visit. Whether admiring its majestic beauty from afar or feeling its misty spray up close, a visit to Wailua Falls is sure to be a highlight of any trip to Kauai.

7.3 Hidden Gems of Kauai

As you traverse the emerald landscapes of Kauai, you'll quickly realize that this island holds far more than meets the eye. Beyond the well-trodden paths and popular attractions lie hidden gems waiting to be discovered, each more enchanting and captivating than the last. These secluded wonders offer a glimpse into the untouched beauty of Kauai, where nature's secrets are whispered through rustling leaves and tumbling waterfalls.

Secret Beaches
Peel back the curtain of palm-fringed shores, and you'll uncover a world of hidden beaches tucked away along Kauai's coastline. From the secluded coves

of Polihale State Park to the serene sands of Hanalei Bay, these untouched stretches of paradise offer solitude and serenity amidst the crashing waves and golden sands. Venture off the beaten path, and you'll be rewarded with the soft whisper of the ocean breeze and the gentle lullaby of the surf, a tranquil oasis far from the crowds.

Mystical Waterfalls

Follow the winding paths that lead into Kauai's verdant interior, and you'll stumble upon hidden waterfalls that seem plucked from the pages of a fairy tale. Tucked away in lush valleys and shaded grottos, these mystical cascades beckon with their shimmering pools and ethereal beauty. Whether you're chasing the thundering roar of Wailua Falls or seeking solace in the secluded embrace of Secret Falls, each waterfall holds its own secrets, waiting to be unraveled by those willing to explore.

Sacred Sites

Venture into the heart of Kauai's rainforest, and you'll discover sacred sites that speak to the island's rich cultural heritage. From ancient heiaus shrouded in mist to sacred groves where the spirits of the land are said to dwell, these hallowed grounds offer a glimpse into the island's storied past. Walk in the footsteps of the ancients as you pay homage to the gods and goddesses who have watched over Kauai for centuries, their presence palpable in the whispering winds and rustling leaves.

Hidden Trails

Step off the well-worn paths and onto the hidden trails that wind their way through Kauai's wilderness, and you'll find yourself immersed in a world of natural wonder and untamed beauty. Whether you're trekking through the lush valleys of the Na Pali Coast or navigating the rugged terrain of Waimea Canyon, each trail offers a chance to connect with the land in a profound and meaningful way. Lose yourself in the quiet solitude of the forest, where the only sounds are the chirping of birds and the rustling of leaves, and let the spirit of Kauai guide you on your journey.

Off-the-Beaten-Path Adventures

For the adventurous souls seeking thrills beyond the tourist hotspots, Kauai offers a wealth of off-the-beaten-path adventures waiting to be experienced. From kayaking down the Wailua River to exploring the hidden sea caves along the Napali Coast, these adrenaline-fueled excursions promise excitement and exhilaration at every turn. Strap on your hiking boots, grab your snorkel gear, and prepare to embark on the adventure of a lifetime as you uncover the hidden gems of Kauai, one thrilling experience at a time.

7.4 Exploring Kauai's Regions

As you embark on your adventure to Kauai, prepare to be captivated by the island's rich tapestry of landscapes and experiences, each region offering its own unique blend of beauty and charm. From the lush valleys of the interior to the sun-kissed shores of the coast, Kauai invites you to explore its diverse regions and uncover the secrets that lie within.

North Shore

Venture to Kauai's North Shore, where verdant mountains meet the sparkling sea in a breathtaking display of natural beauty. Here, you'll find the quaint town of Hanalei, nestled in a lush valley surrounded by towering peaks and cascading waterfalls. Stroll along Hanalei Bay, where gentle waves lap against golden sands, or hike the nearby Napali Coast Trail for sweeping views of rugged cliffs and turquoise waters. Don't miss the chance to visit the iconic Hanalei Pier at sunset, where the sky explodes in a riot of color, casting a magical glow over the landscape.

East Side

Journey to Kauai's East Side, where lush rainforests and fertile valleys beckon with promises of adventure and discovery. Explore the historic town of Kapaa, where charming boutiques and local eateries line the streets, or venture inland to the majestic Wailua River, where waterfalls cascade into tranquil pools hidden among the jungle foliage. Embark on a kayak adventure down the river to the iconic Fern Grotto, a natural amphitheater adorned with hanging ferns and lush vegetation, where the echoes of Hawaiian chants still linger in the air.

South Shore

Discover the sun-drenched shores of Kauai's South Shore, where pristine beaches and crystal-clear waters await. Relax on the powdery sands of Poipu Beach, where gentle waves and warm breezes create the perfect backdrop for a day of sun-soaked bliss, or explore the underwater world at Lawai Beach, renowned for its vibrant coral reefs and abundant marine life. For the adventurous traveler, head inland to explore the rugged terrain of Allerton Garden, where towering trees and exotic plants create a lush oasis amidst the arid landscape.

West Side

Uncover the wild beauty of Kauai's West Side, where dramatic cliffs and sweeping vistas offer a glimpse into the island's untamed wilderness. Marvel at the sheer magnitude of Waimea Canyon, often referred to as the "Grand Canyon of the Pacific," where colorful rock formations and cascading waterfalls create a landscape unlike any other. Explore the charming town of Hanapepe, where historic storefronts and vibrant murals paint a picture of days gone by, or venture to the remote beaches of Polihale State Park, where miles of golden sands stretch as far as the eye can see.

Interior

Delve into the heart of Kauai's interior, where lush valleys and misty mountains beckon with promises of adventure and exploration. Embark on a journey through the enchanting landscapes of Kokee State Park, where verdant forests and panoramic viewpoints offer a glimpse into the island's natural beauty. Hike the trails of Alakai Swamp, home to a diverse array of plant and animal species found nowhere else on earth, or marvel at the majestic beauty of Waialeale, one of the wettest spots on earth, where waterfalls cascade down sheer cliffs in a symphony of sound and motion.

7.5 Dining and Nightlife in Kauai

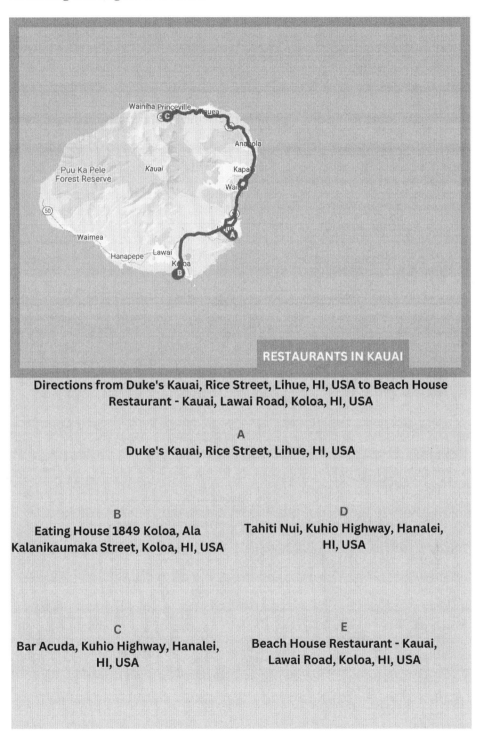

Directions from Duke's Kauai, Rice Street, Lihue, HI, USA to Beach House Restaurant - Kauai, Lawai Road, Koloa, HI, USA

A
Duke's Kauai, Rice Street, Lihue, HI, USA

B
Eating House 1849 Koloa, Ala Kalanikaumaka Street, Koloa, HI, USA

D
Tahiti Nui, Kuhio Highway, Hanalei, HI, USA

C
Bar Acuda, Kuhio Highway, Hanalei, HI, USA

E
Beach House Restaurant - Kauai, Lawai Road, Koloa, HI, USA

As the sun dips below the horizon, casting hues of orange and pink across the shimmering waters of Kauai, a vibrant energy awakens on the island. Amidst the swaying palms and gentle ocean breeze, a culinary adventure awaits, where flavors from around the world converge with the rich traditions of Hawaiian cuisine. From seaside eateries with panoramic ocean views to hidden gems nestled in historic towns, Kauai's dining and nightlife scene offers a tapestry of experiences that tantalize the senses and leave a lasting impression. Join me on a journey through five diverse locales, each offering a unique glimpse into the island's culinary landscape and vibrant nightlife, where every bite and sip tells a story of aloha and hospitality.

The Beach House Restaurant

The Beach House Restaurant offers a dining experience that seamlessly blends breathtaking ocean views with exquisite cuisine. Located on the island's South Shore, this iconic eatery is renowned for its fresh seafood dishes and innovative Pacific Rim-inspired menu. Indulge in local favorites such as macadamia nut-crusted mahi-mahi or coconut shrimp, paired with handcrafted cocktails and fine wines from around the world. As the sun dips below the horizon, diners are treated to a spectacular sunset vista, making every meal at The Beach House an unforgettable experience. Open for lunch and dinner, reservations are recommended to secure a coveted spot overlooking the ocean.

Duke's Kauai

Situated in the heart of Lihue, Duke's Kauai pays homage to legendary surfer Duke Kahanamoku with its laid-back atmosphere and mouthwatering Hawaiian-inspired cuisine. Named after the iconic waterman himself, this waterfront restaurant offers panoramic views of Kalapaki Bay and a menu filled with island favorites such as kalua pork nachos, fresh fish tacos, and signature mai tais. Guests can dine al fresco on the spacious lanai or relax in the casual indoor dining area adorned with surf memorabilia and historic photos of Duke.

With live music and hula dancing most nights, Duke's Kauai provides the perfect setting for a memorable evening on the island. Open for lunch and dinner, with happy hour specials available daily.

Eating House 1849

Step back in time at Eating House 1849, a culinary gem located in the historic town of Kapaa. Named after one of Hawaii's first restaurants, this charming eatery offers a modern twist on classic plantation cuisine, showcasing the diverse flavors and ingredients of the islands. Helmed by renowned chef Roy Yamaguchi, the menu features innovative dishes such as ahi poke bowls, loco moco burgers, and pineapple upside-down cake, all crafted with locally sourced ingredients and seasonal produce. With its rustic decor and warm hospitality, Eating House 1849 invites guests to savor the flavors of Hawaii's past while embracing the spirit of aloha. Open for dinner, reservations are recommended for a truly authentic dining experience.

Bar Acuda

Tucked away in the quaint town of Hanalei on Kauai's North Shore, Bar Acuda offers a sophisticated dining experience that celebrates the flavors of the Mediterranean with a tropical twist. Set in a stylish and intimate atmosphere, this tapas-style restaurant features an array of small plates and shareable dishes crafted from locally sourced ingredients and seasonal produce. Savor the flavors of Spain and Italy with dishes like crispy brussels sprouts, seared scallops, and grilled lamb chops, paired with handcrafted cocktails and a curated selection of wines from around the world. With its cozy ambiance and impeccable service, Bar Acuda provides the perfect setting for a romantic evening or intimate gathering with friends. Open for dinner only, reservations are highly recommended.

Tahiti Nui

Immerse yourself in the vibrant culture of Hawaii at Tahiti Nui, a beloved institution located in the heart of Hanalei. This iconic restaurant and lounge has been serving up island hospitality since 1963, offering a lively atmosphere, live music, and a menu filled with classic Hawaiian comfort food. Feast on local favorites such as kalua pork, fresh fish tacos, and coconut shrimp, washed down with tropical cocktails and ice-cold beers. With its retro decor and friendly staff, Tahiti Nui embodies the laid-back spirit of Kauai's North Shore, making it a favorite hangout for locals and visitors alike. Open for lunch and dinner, with live music performances most nights and a late-night bar scene that keeps the party going until the early hours.

CHAPTER 8
IMMERSING IN HAWAIIAN CULTURE

8.1 Festivals and Events

Hawaii is a melting pot of cultures, traditions, and vibrant celebrations that captivate the hearts and souls of visitors from around the world. Throughout the year, the islands come alive with a tapestry of festivals and events that offer a glimpse into Hawaii's rich heritage and cultural tapestry. Each festival and event is a testament to the resilience of Hawaiian traditions and the enduring legacy of the islands' indigenous people. From the rhythmic sway of hula dancers to the aromatic allure of Kona coffee, Hawaii's festivals offer a sensory feast for the soul.

Merrie Monarch Festival
The Merrie Monarch Festival, held annually in April in Hilo on the Big Island of Hawaii, stands as a vibrant celebration of hula, Hawaiian culture, and traditions. Established in 1963 in honor of King David Kalakaua, who was fondly known as the "Merrie Monarch," this festival has become one of the most

prestigious hula competitions globally. To attend this captivating event, visitors can fly into Hilo International Airport, which is conveniently located just a few miles from the festival venue. While there is typically an entry fee for attending the various performances and competitions, the experience of witnessing the graceful movements of hula dancers amidst the backdrop of traditional chants and music is priceless.

The Merrie Monarch Festival holds profound historical and cultural significance, serving as a platform for perpetuating and showcasing the art of hula. It is a testament to the resilience and preservation of Hawaiian traditions despite the influences of modernity. Apart from the main competition, visitors can explore craft fairs, cultural exhibitions, and educational workshops that delve into the intricacies of Hawaiian arts and crafts.

Aloha Festivals

The Aloha Festivals, spanning the entire month of September across various islands in Hawaii, epitomize the spirit of aloha and the diverse cultural heritage of the Hawaiian archipelago. Dating back to 1946, these festivals aim to honor Hawaii's unique traditions while fostering a sense of community and inclusivity. Traveling to Hawaii during the Aloha Festivals is an opportunity to immerse oneself in a tapestry of events, including parades, concerts, craft fairs, and cultural demonstrations. With events scattered throughout the islands, visitors have the flexibility to experience the festivities wherever they may be staying. Attending the Aloha Festivals provides visitors with a unique opportunity to engage with the local community, learn about Hawaiian customs, and participate in celebrations that have been cherished for generations. It's a chance to embrace the aloha spirit and forge lasting memories against the backdrop of Hawaii's breathtaking landscapes.

Hawaii Food & Wine Festival

For epicureans and culinary enthusiasts, the Hawaii Food & Wine Festival, held annually in October across multiple islands, is a gastronomic extravaganza not to be missed. Established in 2011, this premier culinary event showcases the diverse flavors of Hawaii while highlighting the talents of renowned chefs and winemakers from around the world. Getting to the Hawaii Food & Wine Festival is convenient, with flights available to the various islands hosting events. While ticket prices vary depending on the specific event and package chosen, the opportunity to indulge in gourmet cuisine and exquisite wines amidst stunning island settings is well worth the investment. At the Hawaii Food & Wine Festival, visitors can attend cooking demonstrations, wine tastings, and exclusive dining experiences featuring world-class chefs. It's a chance to savor the essence of Hawaii through its cuisine while mingling with fellow food enthusiasts and industry professionals.

Kona Coffee Cultural Festival

The Kona Coffee Cultural Festival, held annually in November in the historic town of Kailua-Kona on the Big Island, pays homage to Hawaii's prized Kona coffee industry. Since its inception in 1970, this festival has celebrated the rich heritage and cultural significance of Kona coffee, which is renowned worldwide for its exceptional quality and flavor. Visitors can reach Kailua-Kona by flying into Kona International Airport, located just a short drive from the festival venues. While some events may have nominal entry fees, many of the festival's activities, including coffee tastings, farm tours, and cultural exhibits, are often free or offered at minimal cost. The Kona Coffee Cultural Festival serves as a tribute to the generations of farmers who have cultivated coffee in the Kona region for over a century. It offers a glimpse into the labor-intensive process of coffee cultivation, from hand-picking ripe cherries to the meticulous art of roasting and brewing.

Ukulele Festival Hawaii

The Ukulele Festival Hawaii, held annually in July on the island of Oahu, celebrates the enchanting sounds of Hawaii's most iconic musical instrument. Since its inception in 1971, this festival has grown into the largest ukulele festival in the world, attracting thousands of performers and enthusiasts from around the globe. Traveling to Oahu for the Ukulele Festival is straightforward, with flights available to Honolulu International Airport, located near the festival venue. Entry to the festival and its performances is free, making it accessible to all who wish to experience the joyous melodies of the ukulele. The Ukulele Festival Hawaii holds cultural significance by honoring the legacy of this beloved instrument and its role in Hawaiian music and culture. From traditional Hawaiian melodies to contemporary interpretations, the festival showcases the versatility and charm of the ukulele in all its forms.

8.2 Hawaiian Cultural Traditions

Hawaii offers visitors a vibrant tapestry of cultural traditions deeply rooted in the islands' history. Immerse yourself in the authentic spirit of Hawaii by delving into these five diverse cultural practices that continue to shape the identity of the Aloha State.

Hula

Central to Hawaiian culture is the art of hula, a mesmerizing dance form that serves as both a storytelling medium and a means of celebration. Originating from Polynesian settlers, hula encapsulates the essence of Hawaii's folklore, myths, and legends. Visitors have the opportunity to witness captivating hula performances at various cultural events, luaus, and festivals across the islands. Whether it's the graceful movements of hula kahiko (ancient hula) or the modern interpretations of hula auana, each dance carries profound significance, reflecting the island's connection to nature, spirituality, and community.

Lei Making

The lei, a timeless symbol of aloha and hospitality, holds a special place in Hawaiian culture. Traditionally crafted from fresh flowers, leaves, or shells, leis are intricately woven into stunning garlands that adorn the necks of both locals and visitors alike. Engaging in lei making workshops provides a unique opportunity to learn about the significance of different materials and techniques passed down through generations. Beyond its aesthetic appeal, presenting or receiving a lei embodies the spirit of love, respect, and welcome, making it an essential part of any Hawaiian experience.

Lū'au

No visit to Hawaii is complete without attending a lū'au, a festive gathering that showcases the island's culinary delights and cultural heritage. Originating from ancient Hawaiian feasts called 'aha'aina, lū'aus offer an immersive culinary journey featuring traditional dishes such as kalua pig (roast pig), poi (taro paste), lomi lomi salmon, and haupia (coconut pudding). Beyond the tantalizing flavors, lū'aus also feature captivating performances of hula, music, and fire dancing, providing a vibrant glimpse into Hawaiian traditions and hospitality. Whether hosted at resorts, cultural centers, or private gatherings, lū'aus offer an unforgettable experience steeped in the spirit of aloha.

Wayfinding

Wayfinding, the ancient Polynesian art of celestial navigation, represents a profound connection to the natural world and a testament to the seafaring prowess of early Hawaiian voyagers. Rooted in a deep understanding of the stars, ocean currents, winds, and wildlife, wayfinding enabled ancient Hawaiians to navigate vast expanses of the Pacific Ocean with remarkable precision. Today, visitors can embark on voyaging excursions aboard traditional Polynesian voyaging canoes, learning about the techniques and principles of wayfinding firsthand from skilled navigators. By embracing the ancient wisdom of wayfinding, visitors gain a deeper appreciation for Hawaii's maritime heritage and the interconnectedness of nature.

Ho'oponopono

At the heart of Hawaiian culture lies the practice of ho'oponopono, a traditional method of conflict resolution and healing that emphasizes reconciliation and restoration of balance. Rooted in indigenous beliefs and values, ho'oponopono sessions involve open dialogue, forgiveness, and mutual understanding among participants. While historically conducted by kahunas (spiritual leaders), modern interpretations of ho'oponopono focus on fostering harmony within families, communities, and individuals. Visitors seeking a deeper cultural immersion can participate in workshops or retreats led by local practitioners, gaining insights into the transformative power of forgiveness and reconciliation in Hawaiian culture.

8.3 Arts and Music Scene

Hawaii is renowned for its stunning natural beauty, rich cultural heritage, and vibrant arts and music scene. As you embark on a journey to explore this paradise, prepare to be captivated by the diverse array of artistic expressions that thrive within its shores. From traditional Hawaiian hula to contemporary art galleries, Hawaii offers a dynamic tapestry of creative experiences that are sure to enchant visitors from all walks of life.

Honolulu Museum of Art

The Honolulu Museum of Art stands as a beacon of artistic expression in Hawaii. Situated at 900 South Beretania Street, this cultural hub is easily accessible by car, public transportation, or even on foot for those staying nearby. While there is an admission fee for adults, discounts are often available for students, seniors, and military personnel, making it an inclusive destination for all. The museum's significance lies not only in its extensive collection of Asian, European, and American art but also in its dedication to showcasing the diverse cultural heritage of Hawaii. Visitors are transported through time and space as they explore galleries featuring traditional Hawaiian artifacts alongside contemporary works by local artists. The museum's commitment to preserving and promoting indigenous art forms adds depth to its cultural significance, inviting visitors to engage with the history and traditions of the islands.

Waikiki Shell Concert Venue

Located in the iconic Waikiki neighborhood of Honolulu, the Waikiki Shell concert venue is a beloved gathering place for music enthusiasts from near and far. Situated at 2805 Monsarrat Avenue within Kapiolani Park, the venue is easily accessible by car or public transportation, with ample parking available nearby for those driving. Historically, the Waikiki Shell has hosted a diverse array of musical acts, ranging from local Hawaiian artists to international superstars. Its significance as a cultural landmark stems not only from its role in shaping Hawaii's music scene but also from its status as a symbol of community and connection. For visitors, attending a concert at the Waikiki Shell offers a unique opportunity to experience the spirit of aloha through the universal language of music.

Bishop Museum

Situated in the historic district of Kapalama in Honolulu, the Bishop Museum stands as a testament to Hawaii's rich cultural heritage. Located at 1525 Bernice Street, the museum is easily accessible by car or public transportation, with parking available on-site for visitors. While there is an admission fee for adults, discounts are often available for children, seniors, and military personnel, making it an affordable destination for families and individuals alike. The museum's extensive collection of artifacts, artworks, and archival materials offers a comprehensive overview of Hawaiian history, from ancient times to the present day. Founded in 1889 by Charles Reed Bishop in honor of his late wife, Princess Bernice Pauahi Bishop, the museum has played a pivotal role in preserving and perpetuating Hawaiian culture. Its significance lies not only in its vast collection but also in its commitment to community outreach and education. Through exhibitions, programs, and special events, the Bishop Museum serves as a hub for cultural exchange and dialogue, fostering a deeper understanding of Hawaii's past, present, and future.

Donkey Mill Art Center
The Donkey Mill Art Center is a hidden gem for artists and art enthusiasts alike. Located at 78-6670 Mamalahoa Highway, the center is easily accessible by car, with ample parking available on-site for visitors. Historically, the Donkey Mill Art Center has served as a hub for artistic innovation and collaboration in West Hawaii. Its significance lies not only in its role as a cultural institution but also in its commitment to sustainability and stewardship of the land. The center's eco-friendly practices, including rainwater catchment and solar power, reflect its dedication to environmental responsibility. Visitors to the art center can explore galleries featuring works by local and visiting artists, attend workshops and classes, and participate in community events and festivals. From ceramics and printmaking to painting and photography, there's something for everyone to enjoy. Whether creating art or simply appreciating it, the Donkey Mill Art Center offers a unique opportunity to connect with Hawaii's vibrant creative community.

Hilo Palace Theater
Located in the heart of downtown Hilo on the Big Island of Hawaii, the Hilo Palace Theater is a historic landmark and cultural institution beloved by locals and visitors alike. Situated at 38 Haili Street, the theater is easily accessible by car or public transportation, with parking available nearby for patrons. While entry fees vary depending on the event and seating selection, the experience of

attending a performance at the Hilo Palace Theater is well worth the cost. Originally built in 1925 as a vaudeville and silent movie theater, the venue has undergone extensive renovations over the years to preserve its historic charm while accommodating modern audiences. Visitors to the theater can enjoy performances by local artists and touring acts, as well as film screenings and community events. With its intimate atmosphere and welcoming staff, the Hilo Palace Theater provides a memorable experience for audiences of all ages. Whether enjoying a classic film or discovering new talent, a visit to the theater is sure to be a highlight of any trip to Hilo.

8.4 Luau and Traditional Hawaiian Cuisine

Hawaii's culinary scene is a vibrant tapestry woven with the rich flavors of its multicultural heritage. From succulent kalua pig to refreshing poi, the islands offer a feast for the senses that reflects the diverse influences of Hawaiian, Polynesian, Asian, and Western cuisines. One of the best ways to experience the traditional flavors of Hawaii is by attending a luau, where visitors can savor a variety of classic dishes while immersing themselves in the islands' vibrant culture and hospitality.

Old Lahaina Luau
The Old Lahaina Luau is renowned for its authentic portrayal of Hawaiian culture and cuisine. Held at 1251 Front Street, the luau offers a stunning oceanfront setting that sets the stage for an unforgettable evening of food and entertainment. While ticket prices vary depending on seating options and age, the experience is well worth the cost for the feast and cultural performances provided. Visitors to the Old Lahaina Luau can expect to indulge in traditional Hawaiian dishes such as kalua pig, lomi salmon, and poi, all prepared with care and authenticity. The luau's commitment to using locally sourced ingredients ensures that each dish is fresh, flavorful, and reflective of the islands' culinary

heritage. In addition to the delicious food, guests are treated to live music, hula performances, and storytelling that celebrate Hawaii's rich cultural traditions.

Paradise Cove Luau

Located on the western shore of Oahu in Ko Olina, the Paradise Cove Luau is a favorite among visitors seeking a taste of Hawaiian hospitality and cuisine. Situated at 92-1089 Alii Nui Drive, the luau boasts a picturesque seaside setting that provides the perfect backdrop for an evening of festivities. While ticket prices vary depending on package options and age, the experience includes a lavish buffet dinner and a variety of cultural activities and entertainment. Guests at the Paradise Cove Luau can feast on an array of traditional Hawaiian dishes, including kalua pig, poi, and haupia, all served with a side of island hospitality. The luau's beachside location offers a serene setting for dining and entertainment, with stunning views of the Pacific Ocean and nightly sunsets that add to the ambiance. In addition to the delicious food, guests can participate in activities such as lei making, coconut husking, and hula lessons, providing hands-on experiences that deepen their appreciation for Hawaiian culture.

Feast at Lele Luau: Situated in the historic town of Lahaina on Maui's west coast, the Feast at Lele Luau offers a unique dining experience that celebrates the culinary traditions of Hawaii and Polynesia. Located at 505 Front Street, the luau distinguishes itself with its gourmet four-course dinner served tableside, providing a more intimate and luxurious dining experience for guests. While ticket prices are higher compared to traditional buffet-style luaus, the Feast at Lele offers a premium culinary experience that's well worth the cost. Guests at the Feast at Lele Luau are treated to a culinary journey through the Pacific Islands, with each course highlighting the flavors and ingredients of a different region. From Hawaiian imu-roasted pig to Tahitian poisson cru, the menu showcases the diverse culinary traditions of Polynesia with creativity and finesse. In addition to the exquisite food, guests are entertained by cultural performances that transport them to the islands of Hawaii, Samoa, Tahiti, and New Zealand, providing a truly immersive dining experience.

Hale Koa Hotel Luau: The Hale Koa Hotel Luau offers a family-friendly dining experience that showcases the flavors and traditions of Hawaii. Located at 2055 Kalia Road, the luau takes place on the hotel's oceanfront lawn, providing a picturesque setting for an evening of food and entertainment. While ticket prices vary depending on age and military affiliation, the luau offers an affordable option for visitors looking to experience Hawaiian culture. Guests at the Hale Koa Hotel Luau can feast on a buffet-style dinner featuring classic Hawaiian dishes such as kalua pig, chicken long rice, and haupia, all served with a side of island hospitality. The luau's entertainment lineup includes hula performances, live music, and fire dancing, providing entertainment for guests of all ages. Additionally, the Hale Koa Hotel Luau offers cultural activities such as lei making and ukulele lessons, allowing guests to immerse themselves in Hawaiian traditions.

Drums of the Pacific Luau: Located at the Hyatt Regency Maui Resort and Spa in Kaanapali, the Drums of the Pacific Luau offers a dynamic and interactive dining experience that celebrates the music, dance, and cuisine of Hawaii and Polynesia. Situated at 200 Nohea Kai Drive, the luau takes place on the resort's oceanfront lawn, providing breathtaking views of the Pacific Ocean and the neighboring islands of Lanai and Molokai. While ticket prices vary depending on age and seating options, the luau offers an all-inclusive package that includes dinner and entertainment. Guests at the Drums of the Pacific Luau can enjoy a buffet-style dinner featuring a variety of Hawaiian and Polynesian dishes, including kalua pig, poi, and mahi-mahi, all served with a side of island hospitality. The luau's entertainment lineup includes traditional hula performances, fire dancing, and live music, providing a captivating glimpse into the cultural traditions of the Pacific Islands.

CHAPTER 9
OUTDOOR ADVENTURES

9.1 Hiking Trails and Nature Walks

Hawaii offers an array of outdoor adventures for enthusiasts and nature lovers alike. Among its myriad attractions, the hiking trails and nature walks stand out as quintessential experiences that capture the essence of Hawaii's natural beauty. Here, we delve into five captivating destinations that promise unforgettable outdoor adventures.

Kalalau Trail, Na Pali Coast State Park
Along the rugged Na Pali Coast on the island of Kauai, the Kalalau Trail is a breathtaking trek that winds through verdant valleys, towering sea cliffs, and pristine beaches. Spanning 11 miles one way, this challenging trail rewards hikers with awe-inspiring vistas of the Pacific Ocean and lush rainforest landscapes. The trailhead begins at Ke'e Beach and culminates at Kalalau

Beach, where intrepid adventurers can camp beneath the stars. While the trail remains open year-round, it is advisable to embark on the journey during the drier months of May to September to avoid inclement weather. No entry fee is required, but permits are necessary for camping, obtainable through the Hawaii State Parks website.

Diamond Head Summit Trail

Located just a short drive from Waikiki on the island of Oahu, the Diamond Head Summit Trail offers a relatively easy yet rewarding hike with panoramic views of Honolulu and the sparkling Pacific Ocean. Rising 762 feet above sea level, the trail ascends through a series of switchbacks and tunnels to reach the historic summit lookout. Built in the early 1900s as a military observation station, the trail showcases remnants of its storied past, including bunkers and artillery platforms. Open daily from 6:00 AM to 6:00 PM, visitors can access the trail via bus, car, or organized tours. An entry fee of $5 per vehicle or $1 per pedestrian is required for non-residents, making it an affordable and accessible adventure for all.

Haleakalā Crater Trail

Perched atop the summit of Maui's dormant volcano, Haleakalā Crater Trail beckons travelers to explore an otherworldly landscape of lunar-like terrain and vibrant cinder cones. Spanning approximately 11 miles round trip, the trail leads adventurers into the heart of the crater, where they can witness the ethereal beauty of sunrise or sunset casting hues of orange and pink across the horizon. While the trail remains open year-round, visitors are encouraged to check weather conditions and trail status before embarking on the journey. Entry to Haleakalā National Park requires a $30 per vehicle fee or $15 per pedestrian, valid for three days. Shuttle services are available for those seeking transportation to the summit, offering convenience and ease of access for visitors.

Manoa Falls Trail

Immerse yourself in the lush rainforest of Oahu's Manoa Valley as you embark on the enchanting Manoa Falls Trail. Located just a short drive from downtown Honolulu, this leisurely hike meanders through a verdant canopy of bamboo groves, towering banyan trees, and fragrant ginger flowers. Spanning approximately 1.6 miles round trip, the trail culminates at the base of Manoa Falls, a 150-foot cascade plunging into a tranquil pool below. Open daily from dawn to dusk, the trail offers a refreshing escape from the hustle and bustle of urban life. While no entry fee is required, visitors are encouraged to practice Leave No Trace principles and respect the natural environment during their visit.

Waimea Canyon Trail

Dubbed the "Grand Canyon of the Pacific," Waimea Canyon on the island of Kauai boasts a network of hiking trails that showcase the dramatic beauty of its crimson cliffs and lush valleys. The Waimea Canyon Trail offers a moderate trek with panoramic viewpoints overlooking the sprawling canyon and distant waterfalls. Spanning approximately 3.4 miles round trip, the trail provides opportunities for birdwatching, photography, and exploration of the canyon's geological wonders. Open year-round, visitors can access the trail via car or organized tours, with no entry fee required for exploration. As one of Hawaii's most iconic natural landmarks, Waimea Canyon epitomizes the awe-inspiring beauty of the islands and offers a captivating glimpse into the geological history of the Pacific region.

9.2 Snorkeling and Scuba Diving Spots

Hawaii offers an array of exhilarating snorkeling and scuba diving spots that beckon adventure seekers from around the globe. Immerse yourself in the crystal-clear waters of the Pacific Ocean and explore an underwater world teeming with colorful coral reefs, fascinating marine creatures, and captivating underwater landscapes. Here, we delve into five must-visit snorkeling and scuba diving spots in Hawaii, each offering a unique and unforgettable aquatic experience.

Hanauma Bay Nature Preserve

Located on the southeastern coast of Oahu, Hanauma Bay Nature Preserve is a marine sanctuary renowned for its spectacular coral reefs and diverse marine life. Open daily from 6:00 AM to 7:00 PM, this breathtaking natural wonder welcomes visitors with its tranquil turquoise waters and pristine white sandy beach. To reach Hanauma Bay, visitors can opt for a scenic drive along the Kalanianaole Highway or take advantage of the convenient shuttle service available from Waikiki. While there is an entry fee of $12.50 per person, the experience of snorkeling amidst vibrant coral gardens and encountering tropical fish species such as parrotfish, butterflyfish, and moray eels is truly priceless. Hanauma Bay also holds significant cultural importance, serving as a traditional fishing and gathering site for native Hawaiians. Visitors are encouraged to respect the preservation efforts and guidelines set forth by the nature preserve to ensure the conservation of its delicate marine ecosystem.

Molokini Crater

Situated just off the coast of Maui, Molokini Crater is a partially submerged volcanic crater renowned for its exceptional snorkeling and scuba diving opportunities. This crescent-shaped islet, formed over 150,000 years ago, boasts crystal-clear waters and an abundance of marine life, making it a must-visit destination for underwater enthusiasts. Molokini Crater is accessible via boat tours departing from Maalaea Harbor or Kihei Boat Ramp. Most tours operate in the morning, typically departing between 7:00 AM and 8:00 AM, allowing visitors to enjoy optimal visibility and encounter an array of marine species, including reef sharks, manta rays, and vibrant coral formations. While tour prices vary depending on the operator and package selected, the experience of snorkeling or scuba diving within the crater's protected marine sanctuary is nothing short of extraordinary. Moreover, Molokini holds cultural significance as a sacred site in Hawaiian mythology, adding an enriching dimension to the overall experience.

Kealakekua Bay

Kealakekua Bay is a marine sanctuary revered for its pristine waters, vibrant coral reefs, and historical significance. Captain James Cook's first encounter with the Hawaiian Islands took place at this idyllic bay in 1779, lending it a profound historical legacy. Today, Kealakekua Bay remains a popular destination for snorkelers and scuba divers seeking to explore its underwater wonders. Access to Kealakekua Bay is primarily by boat, with numerous tour operators offering guided snorkeling and scuba diving excursions departing from nearby locations such as Kailua-Kona or Keauhou Bay. While there is no entry fee to access the bay, visitors are encouraged to exercise caution and adhere to marine conservation regulations to preserve its ecological integrity. Snorkeling or diving in Kealakekua Bay offers a chance to encounter an array of marine life, including colorful fish, sea turtles, and even spinner dolphins frolicking in the pristine waters.

Kaanapali Beach

Kaanapali Beach, located along Maui's western shore, is not only renowned for its powdery golden sands and breathtaking sunsets but also for its exceptional snorkeling opportunities. This picturesque stretch of coastline boasts calm, clear waters teeming with marine life, making it an ideal spot for both beginners and experienced snorkelers alike. Kaanapali Beach is easily accessible by car and offers ample parking for visitors. Snorkeling at Kaanapali Beach provides the chance to encounter an array of tropical fish species, including tangs, triggerfish, and pufferfish, amidst vibrant coral formations just a short swim from the shore. The beach's proximity to luxury resorts and amenities ensures visitors can enjoy a seamless and comfortable snorkeling experience, with equipment rentals and guided tours readily available. Additionally, Kaanapali Beach holds cultural significance as a historic site where Hawaiian royalty once indulged in leisure activities, adding a fascinating layer of heritage to the overall experience.

Shark's Cove

Situated on the North Shore of Oahu, Shark's Cove is a natural lava-rock formation renowned for its incredible snorkeling opportunities and dramatic underwater landscapes. Despite its ominous name, Shark's Cove is a haven for marine life, offering visitors the chance to explore an underwater maze of lava tubes, caves, and crevices teeming with colorful fish and coral formations. The cove is accessible via a short walk from the parking lot located along Kamehameha Highway. While there is no entry fee to access Shark's Cove, visitors should exercise caution when entering the water, especially during high surf conditions. Snorkelers can expect to encounter a diverse array of marine species, including Hawaiian green sea turtles, octopuses, and elusive reef sharks, amidst the cove's crystal-clear waters. Moreover, Shark's Cove holds cultural significance as a traditional gathering place for native Hawaiians, adding a profound sense of heritage to the snorkeling experience.

9.3 Surfing and Water Sports

Hawaii, with its stunning beaches, crystal-clear waters, and perfect waves, is a haven for outdoor enthusiasts, especially those seeking thrilling water sports adventures. Among the plethora of activities available, surfing and water sports reign supreme, offering visitors an exhilarating and immersive experience in the heart of the Pacific. Let's delve into captivating surf and water sports activities that showcase Hawaii's natural beauty and adrenaline-pumping adventures.

Surfing at Waikiki Beach

Located on the south shore of Oahu, Waikiki Beach is renowned as the birthplace of modern surfing. Its gentle rolling waves and warm waters provide an ideal setting for both beginners and experienced surfers alike. The beach offers consistent surf year-round, making it a favorite spot for surfers from across the globe. Waikiki Beach operates from dawn till dusk, ensuring ample time for visitors to catch the perfect wave. There is no entry fee to access the beach, and various surf rental shops line the shore, offering everything from surfboards to lessons with experienced instructors. Beyond its surfing fame, Waikiki Beach holds historical and cultural significance. Once the playground of Hawaiian royalty, it now boasts a vibrant atmosphere with bustling streets, luxurious resorts, and iconic landmarks like Diamond Head Crater. Visitors can immerse themselves in the rich heritage of Hawaii while enjoying the thrill of riding the waves.

Snorkeling at Hanauma Bay

For those seeking an underwater adventure, Hanauma Bay on the island of Oahu offers unparalleled snorkeling experiences. Nestled within a volcanic crater, this marine sanctuary teems with colorful coral reefs, tropical fish, and other fascinating marine life. Hanauma Bay is open from 6:00 am to 7:00 pm daily, with limited entry to preserve its delicate ecosystem. Visitors are required to pay an entry fee, which includes educational programs on marine conservation and safety guidelines. Snorkeling gear can be rented on-site, ensuring a hassle-free experience for all. Apart from its natural beauty, Hanauma Bay holds cultural significance as a sacred site for Native Hawaiians. It's a place where visitors can connect with the land and sea while learning about the importance of conservation efforts in preserving fragile ecosystems.

Kayaking at Wailua River

Venture to the lush island of Kauai and discover the enchanting Wailua River, where kayaking offers a unique way to explore Hawaii's natural wonders. Paddling along the tranquil waters of the Wailua River, visitors are treated to breathtaking views of lush valleys, cascading waterfalls, and verdant landscapes. Wailua River is accessible year-round, with kayak rental facilities available near the river's mouth. Guided tours are also offered, providing insight into the area's history, flora, and fauna. The river is typically open from sunrise to sunset, allowing ample time for exploration. Beyond its scenic beauty, Wailua River holds historical significance as a sacred site and the ancient capital of Kauai. Visitors can paddle to the iconic Fern Grotto, a natural lava rock formation adorned with lush ferns and native foliage, adding a touch of mystique to the adventure.

Surfing at Banzai Pipeline

For experienced surfers seeking an adrenaline rush, the Banzai Pipeline on the North Shore of Oahu beckons with its legendary waves and thrilling surf breaks. Known for its massive swells and hollow barrels, this iconic surf spot has earned a reputation as one of the most challenging and exhilarating breaks in the world. Surfing at Banzai Pipeline is best during the winter months when the North Shore comes alive with colossal waves. While the waves may be intimidating for beginners, spectators can marvel at the skill and bravery of seasoned surfers tackling the legendary barrels from the safety of the shore. Banzai Pipeline holds cultural significance as a sacred place for Native Hawaiians, who regard the ocean as a source of life and spirituality. Visitors can witness the power and beauty of the sea while paying homage to the ancient traditions and wisdom passed down through generations.

Snorkeling with Manta Rays

Embark on a mesmerizing underwater journey at Kealakekua Bay on the Big Island of Hawaii, where snorkeling with majestic manta rays offers a once-in-a-lifetime experience. As night falls, these graceful creatures emerge from the depths, gliding gracefully through the water in search of plankton. Snorkeling tours to Kealakekua Bay typically depart in the evening, allowing visitors to witness the awe-inspiring sight of manta rays feeding under the moonlit sky. Experienced guides lead the way, providing safety instructions and insights into the behavior and conservation of these gentle giants. Kealakekua Bay holds historical significance as the site where Captain James Cook first landed in Hawaii in 1778, forever altering the course of Hawaiian history. Visitors can snorkel amidst vibrant coral reefs and tropical fish while reflecting on the rich tapestry of culture and exploration that defines Hawaii's past.

9.4 Ziplining and Eco-Tours

Embark on a thrilling journey through Hawaii's lush landscapes and soaring canopies with exhilarating ziplining and eco-tours. From the verdant rainforests of Hilo to the rugged cliffs of Maui, these immersive experiences offer a unique perspective on the Aloha State's natural wonders. Here, we delve into must-see destinations that promise adrenaline-pumping adventures and eco-friendly exploration.

Kohala Zipline

Kohala Zipline offers an unforgettable ziplining adventure through towering trees and cascading waterfalls. Located approximately 30 minutes from Waimea, this eco-friendly attraction features eight exhilarating ziplines that traverse lush valleys and pristine streams. Open daily from 8:00 AM to 5:00 PM, visitors can access Kohala Zipline via car or organized tours. Admission prices start at $169 per person, with discounts available for children and groups. As one of the island's premier ziplining destinations, Kohala Zipline combines adrenaline-fueled thrills with breathtaking vistas of Hawaii's diverse landscapes.

Skyline Eco-Adventures

Embark on a high-flying adventure above the lush forests of Maui with Skyline Eco-Adventures, Hawaii's first zipline company. Located on the slopes of Haleakalā in upcountry Maui, this award-winning attraction offers adrenaline-pumping ziplines that soar above the treetops and ravines of the scenic landscape. Open daily from 8:00 AM to 5:00 PM, visitors can reach Skyline Eco-Adventures via car or shuttle service from various locations on the island. Admission prices start at $159 per person, with discounts available for online bookings and group packages. With a commitment to environmental sustainability and cultural preservation, Skyline Eco-Adventures provides a thrilling yet eco-conscious way to experience the beauty of Maui's natural surroundings.

Kauai Backcountry Adventures

Embark on a journey through the heart of Kauai's lush interior with Kauai Backcountry Adventures, offering ziplining tours through the island's historic irrigation channels and tropical forests. Located in Hanamaulu, just minutes from Lihue Airport, this eco-friendly attraction features ziplines that traverse verdant valleys and scenic waterways. Open daily from 7:30 AM to 4:00 PM, visitors can access Kauai Backcountry Adventures via car or shuttle service from nearby accommodations. Admission prices start at $145 per person, with discounts available for children and group bookings. As you soar through the canopy, you'll gain insight into the rich history and cultural significance of Kauai's irrigation systems, known as "auwai," which have sustained the island's communities for centuries.

Umauma Falls Zipline and Rappel Experience

Embark on an adrenaline-fueled adventure in the lush rainforests of the Hamakua Coast with Umauma Falls Zipline and Rappel Experience on the Big Island. Located just north of Hilo, this thrilling attraction offers ziplines that traverse lush valleys and soar above cascading waterfalls, providing breathtaking views of Hawaii's iconic landscapes. Open daily from 8:00 AM to 5:00 PM, visitors can access Umauma Falls Zipline via car or shuttle service from Hilo and surrounding areas. Admission prices start at $189 per person, with discounts available for online bookings and group packages. As you zip through the canopy, you'll have the opportunity to rappel down a waterfall and swim in the natural pools below, immersing yourself in the beauty and tranquility of Hawaii's tropical paradise.

Climb Works Keana Farms

Experience the thrill of ziplining above the North Shore's lush farmland with Climb Works Keana Farms on Oahu. Located just 45 minutes from Waikiki, this family-friendly attraction offers ziplines that traverse verdant valleys and panoramic ocean views, providing a unique perspective on Oahu's diverse landscapes. Open daily from 8:00 AM to 5:00 PM, visitors can access Climb Works Keana Farms via car or shuttle service from Honolulu and surrounding areas. Admission prices start at $169 per person, with discounts available for online bookings and group packages. As you soar through the air, you'll learn about the rich agricultural heritage of Oahu's North Shore and the sustainable farming practices that sustain the island's communities.

CHAPTER 10
TRAVELING WITH SPECIAL INTERESTS

10.1 Family-Friendly Activities

Hawaii, often celebrated for its natural beauty and adventurous spirit, also offers a plethora of family-friendly activities that cater to travelers of all ages. From interactive cultural experiences to thrilling outdoor adventures, the islands abound with opportunities for families to create lasting memories together. Here, we delve into five must-visit family-friendly activities in Hawaii, each offering a unique blend of fun, education, and cultural enrichment.

Polynesian Cultural Center
The Polynesian Cultural Center stands as a living museum dedicated to preserving and sharing the diverse cultures of Polynesia. Open daily from 12:00 PM to 9:00 PM, this expansive cultural complex offers immersive experiences and entertaining performances that showcase the traditions of Hawaii, Samoa,

Tahiti, Fiji, and other Pacific Island nations. To reach the Polynesian Cultural Center, visitors can embark on a scenic drive from Honolulu or take advantage of shuttle services available from Waikiki. While there is an entry fee for access to the center, various packages are available that include cultural demonstrations, luau feasts, and interactive activities suitable for the whole family. At the Polynesian Cultural Center, families can embark on guided tours of authentic village replicas, participate in hands-on workshops, and witness captivating performances that highlight Polynesian music, dance, and storytelling. From learning the art of fire-making to trying traditional island cuisine, the center offers a wealth of opportunities for cultural immersion and family bonding.

Honolulu Zoo

Situated in the heart of Waikiki, the Honolulu Zoo offers families the chance to encounter exotic wildlife from around the world amidst lush tropical surroundings. Open daily from 9:00 AM to 4:30 PM, this beloved zoological park is home to over 900 animal species, including elephants, giraffes, lions, and endangered Hawaiian native species such as the Nene goose and Hawaiian monk seal. Access to the Honolulu Zoo is convenient, with parking available onsite and easily accessible via public transportation from various parts of the island. While there is an entry fee for adults and children, the zoo offers discounts for Hawaii residents and military personnel. Families visiting the Honolulu Zoo can explore themed exhibits showcasing animals from different regions, participate in educational programs and guided tours, and even enjoy up-close animal encounters and feeding experiences. With its lush botanical gardens, interactive children's play areas, and scenic picnic spots, the zoo provides an engaging and educational experience for visitors of all ages.

Maui Ocean Center

Located on the picturesque island of Maui, the Maui Ocean Center is a world-class aquarium dedicated to showcasing the rich marine life of Hawaii and the Pacific. Open daily from 9:00 AM to 5:00 PM, this award-winning oceanarium offers families the opportunity to explore vibrant coral reefs, encounter rare sea creatures, and learn about marine conservation efforts in the region. To reach the Maui Ocean Center, visitors can drive along the Honoapiilani Highway or take advantage of shuttle services available from nearby resort areas. While there is an entry fee for adults and children, discounted tickets are available for seniors, military personnel, and Hawaii residents. At the Maui Ocean Center, families can marvel at mesmerizing exhibits featuring sharks, rays, turtles, and colorful tropical fish species endemic to Hawaiian waters. Interactive touch pools, educational presentations, and behind-the-scenes tours offer visitors a deeper understanding of marine ecosystems and the importance of protecting ocean habitats. Additionally, the center's commitment to sustainable practices and environmental stewardship aligns with Hawaii's cultural values and conservation ethos.

Kualoa Ranch

Kualoa Ranch offers families the opportunity to embark on a variety of outdoor adventures and cultural experiences. Open daily from 7:30 AM to 5:30 PM, this sprawling nature reserve invites visitors to explore its scenic valleys, verdant forests, and iconic filming locations featured in blockbuster movies and television shows. To reach Kualoa Ranch, visitors can embark on a scenic drive from Honolulu or book transportation through guided tour operators offering round-trip transfers. While there is an entry fee for access to the ranch, various activity packages are available that include guided tours, adventure activities, and cultural demonstrations. At Kualoa Ranch, families can choose from an array of activities suited to their interests and preferences, including horseback riding, ATV tours, zip-lining, and jungle expedition tours. Guided cultural experiences offer insights into Hawaii's rich history and heritage, with opportunities to visit ancient Hawaiian fishponds, sacred temples, and archaeological sites. The ranch's commitment to sustainable tourism and land conservation ensures that future generations can continue to enjoy its pristine natural beauty and cultural significance.

Waikiki Aquarium

Situated along the iconic shores of Waikiki, the Waikiki Aquarium is a family-friendly destination that offers visitors the chance to explore Hawaii's diverse marine ecosystems and learn about ocean conservation. Open daily from 9:00 AM to 4:30 PM, this intimate aquarium showcases a wide range of aquatic species endemic to the Hawaiian Islands and the Pacific region. Access to the Waikiki Aquarium is convenient, with parking available nearby and easily accessible via public transportation from various parts of the island. While there is an entry fee for adults and children, discounted tickets are available for seniors, military personnel, and Hawaii residents. At the Waikiki Aquarium, families can embark on a journey of discovery through interactive exhibits, educational presentations, and guided tours led by marine experts. Highlights include the Hawaiian Monk Seal Habitat, Pacific Coral Reef exhibit, and Hawaiian Green Sea Turtle Lagoon, where visitors can observe these fascinating creatures up close. Special events and programs throughout the year offer additional opportunities for hands-on learning and family fun.

10.2 LGBTQ+ Travel in Hawaii

Hawaii, with its breathtaking landscapes and vibrant culture, is not only a paradise for nature lovers but also a welcoming destination for LGBTQ+ travelers seeking inclusive and memorable experiences. From picturesque beaches to bustling urban hubs, Hawaii offers a diverse array of attractions that cater to the interests and preferences of the LGBTQ+ community. Let's explore must-see LGBTQ+ travel destinations in Hawaii, each offering a unique blend of beauty, history, and acceptance.

Honolulu Pride Festival

Located in the heart of Oahu, Honolulu Pride Festival is a colorful celebration of diversity and equality that attracts LGBTQ+ individuals and allies from across the Hawaiian Islands and beyond. The festival typically takes place in October and features a lively parade, live entertainment, cultural performances, and a variety of vendors showcasing LGBTQ+ arts, crafts, and cuisine. The festival kicks off with the Pride Parade, a dazzling procession of floats, marchers, and performers making their way through the streets of Waikiki. Following the parade, attendees gather at the festival grounds to enjoy live music, dance parties, and community outreach programs promoting LGBTQ+ rights and awareness. Honolulu Pride Festival holds historical significance as a symbol of progress and acceptance in Hawaii's LGBTQ+ community. It provides a platform for LGBTQ+ individuals to celebrate their identities openly and proudly while fostering a sense of unity and solidarity among diverse communities.

Hula's Bar and Lei Stand

Hula's Bar and Lei Stand is a legendary LGBTQ+ hotspot that has been serving up tropical drinks, lively entertainment, and unforgettable memories for over four decades. Situated steps away from Waikiki Beach, Hula's offers stunning ocean views by day and pulsating nightlife by night, making it a must-visit destination for LGBTQ+ travelers. Hula's is open daily from 10:00 am to 2:00 am, welcoming patrons of all ages to enjoy its festive atmosphere and friendly vibes. The bar hosts a variety of events throughout the week, including drag shows, karaoke nights, and themed parties that cater to diverse tastes and interests. With its laid-back ambiance and inclusive ethos, Hula's Bar and Lei Stand holds cultural significance as a gathering place for Hawaii's LGBTQ+

community. It serves as a beacon of acceptance and celebration, where people from all walks of life can come together to share laughter, love, and aloha spirit.

LGBTQ+ Wedding Destinations

Hawaii's stunning landscapes and romantic ambiance make it an ideal destination for LGBTQ+ couples looking to tie the knot in paradise. From lush gardens to pristine beaches, Hawaii offers a plethora of picturesque wedding venues that cater to every couple's vision and budget. Popular LGBTQ+ wedding destinations in Hawaii include the island of Maui, known for its breathtaking sunsets and luxurious resorts, and the island of Kauai, home to secluded beaches and lush rainforests perfect for intimate ceremonies. Oahu, with its vibrant urban scene and historic landmarks, also offers a variety of wedding venues ranging from chic rooftop bars to elegant ballrooms. In addition to its natural beauty, Hawaii holds historical significance as a trailblazer in LGBTQ+ rights and marriage equality. In 2013, Hawaii became one of the first states to legalize same-sex marriage, paving the way for LGBTQ+ couples to exchange vows in a welcoming and inclusive environment.

LGBTQ+ Surf Camps

For LGBTQ+ travelers seeking adventure and camaraderie, LGBTQ+ surf camps offer a unique opportunity to learn to surf or hone their skills in the company of like-minded individuals. Hawaii's world-renowned surf breaks provide the perfect backdrop for an unforgettable surf experience, whether catching waves for the first time or mastering advanced techniques. LGBTQ+ surf camps typically take place on the island of Oahu's North Shore, home to legendary breaks like Waimea Bay and Pipeline. Participants receive personalized instruction from experienced surf coaches and enjoy access to premium surf equipment, ensuring a safe and enjoyable learning experience. Beyond surfing, LGBTQ+ surf camps foster a sense of community and belonging, creating lasting friendships and memories that extend beyond the waves. Participants bond over shared experiences, celebrate each other's successes, and embrace the spirit of aloha that permeates Hawaii's surf culture.

LGBTQ+ Cultural Tours

Immerse yourself in Hawaii's rich history and culture with LGBTQ+ cultural tours that offer a unique perspective on the islands' heritage and traditions. From exploring ancient Hawaiian sites to learning about the contributions of LGBTQ+ individuals to Hawaii's arts and culture, these tours provide insight into the diverse tapestry of Hawaii's past and present. LGBTQ+ cultural tours may include visits to historic sites like Iolani Palace, the former residence of Hawaiian monarchs, or the Bishop Museum, which showcases artifacts and exhibits related to Hawaiian history and culture. Participants also have the opportunity to meet local LGBTQ+ artists, activists, and community leaders who are making a positive impact on Hawaii's LGBTQ+ community. By participating in LGBTQ+ cultural tours, travelers not only gain a deeper understanding of Hawaii's heritage but also contribute to the ongoing dialogue surrounding LGBTQ+ rights and acceptance. These tours promote inclusivity, diversity, and mutual respect, reflecting the spirit of aloha that defines Hawaii's welcoming and inclusive ethos.

CHAPTER 11
PRACTICAL INFORMATION AND TRAVEL RESOURCES

11.1 Maps of Hawaii; Oahu, Maui, Big Island and Kauai

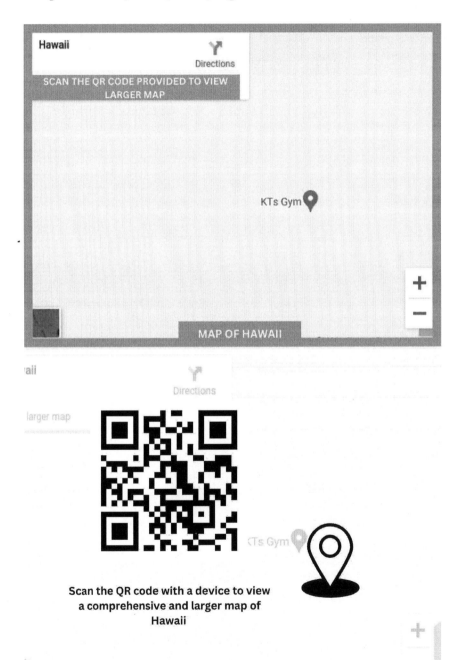

Scan the QR code with a device to view a comprehensive and larger map of Hawaii

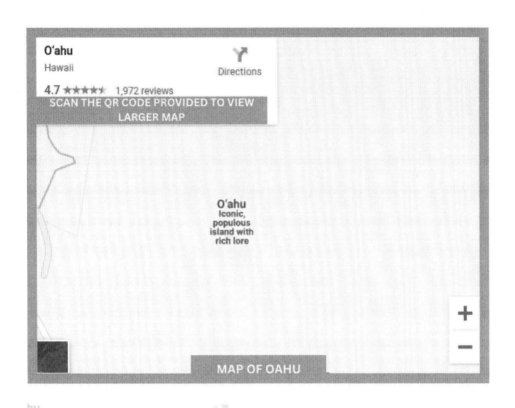

Scan the QR code with a device to view a comprehensive and larger map of Oahu

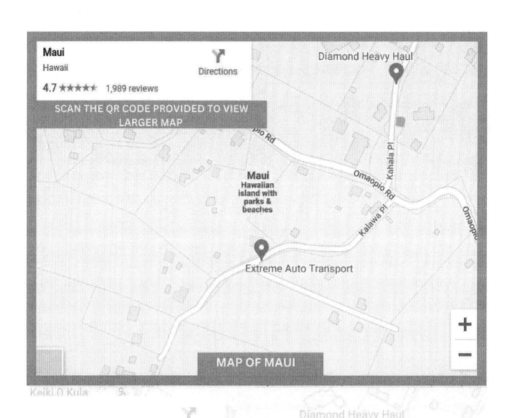

Scan the QR code with a device to view a comprehensive and larger map of Maui

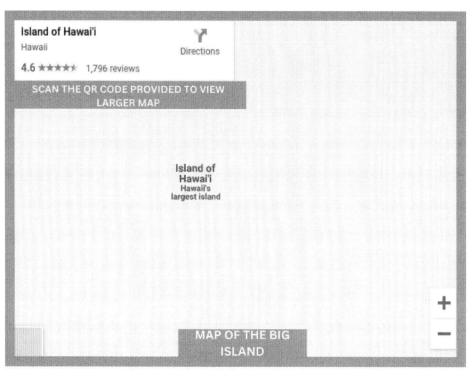

Scan the QR code with a device to view a comprehensive and larger map of the Big Island

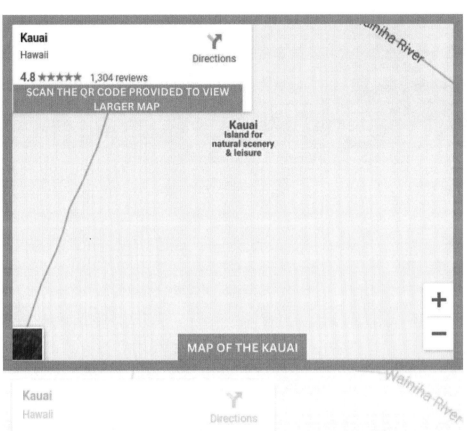

Scan the QR code with a device to view a comprehensive and larger map of Kauai

Hawaii, with its diverse landscapes and unique culture, is a dream destination for many travelers. From the vibrant beaches of Oahu to the lush valleys of Kauai, each island offers its own distinct charm and attractions. Navigating these islands efficiently and safely requires a good understanding of the available maps and navigation tools, both in traditional paper format and digitally.

Hawaii Tourist Map

A Hawaii tourist map serves as an invaluable companion for visitors looking to explore the islands. These maps typically highlight key tourist destinations, scenic routes, hiking trails, beaches, and cultural sites. They are readily available at airports, hotels, tourist information centers, and rental car agencies across the islands. When using a paper map, it's essential to familiarize yourself with the island's geography and key landmarks. This will help you navigate efficiently and make the most of your time exploring the islands. Additionally, always ensure that your map is up-to-date, as roads and attractions may undergo changes over time.

Accessing Offline Maps in Hawaii

For travelers who prefer offline navigation, obtaining a paper map is the way to go. These maps are easily accessible and can be kept in your pocket or car for quick reference. Most rental car companies provide complimentary maps to their customers, but you can also purchase them at convenience stores and souvenir shops.

Alternatively, if you prefer a more detailed and comprehensive map, consider investing in a specialized map book or atlas that covers the entire state of Hawaii. These books often include detailed maps of each island, as well as useful information on points of interest, hiking trails, and recreational activities.

Digital Maps

Navigating Hawaii has never been easier thanks to a variety of digital mapping tools and applications. Whether you're using a smartphone, tablet, or GPS device, there are numerous options available to help you explore the islands with confidence. One of the most popular digital mapping services is Google Maps, which offers detailed maps of Hawaii's roads, trails, and points of interest. Users can easily access turn-by-turn directions, real-time traffic updates, and even offline maps for areas with limited cellular coverage. For those seeking a more specialized navigation experience, consider using dedicated travel apps such as TripAdvisor, Yelp, or AllTrails. These apps provide user-generated reviews, recommendations, and detailed trail maps to help you plan your itinerary and discover hidden gems around the islands.

Accessing Hawaii's Maps Digitally

To access Hawaii's maps digitally, travelers can simply visit the official tourism website or download the Hawaii Visitors and Convention Bureau app. These platforms provide interactive maps, travel guides, and insider tips to help you make the most of your Hawaiian adventure In addition to official tourism resources, many local businesses and attractions also offer digital maps and guides on their websites or social media channels. By following them online and staying connected, you can stay informed about the latest updates, promotions, and events happening around the islands.

11.2 Five Days Itinerary

Embarking on a journey to Hawaii is akin to stepping into a realm of unparalleled natural beauty and cultural richness. Begin your adventure by landing in Oahu, the vibrant heart of the Hawaiian archipelago. Upon arrival, feel the warm embrace of the tropical breeze and the welcoming spirit of Aloha. Dive into the island's diverse culture by immersing yourself in its bustling capital, Honolulu. Spend your first day strolling along the iconic Waikiki Beach, where the azure waters meet the golden sands, and soak in the radiant sunset that paints the sky in hues of orange and pink. As night falls, treat your taste buds to a culinary feast at one of the many local eateries, indulging in traditional Hawaiian dishes like poke and kalua pork.

Day Two: Exploring Oahu's Rich Heritage and Natural Wonders
Embark on a journey of discovery as you delve into Oahu's rich history and breathtaking landscapes. Begin your day with a visit to the Pearl Harbor National Memorial, a poignant reminder of the island's pivotal role in World War II. Pay your respects at the USS Arizona Memorial and immerse yourself in the stories of courage and sacrifice that echo through its halls. Afterward, venture into the lush hinterlands of the island, where emerald valleys and cascading waterfalls await. Take a scenic drive along the North Shore, stopping to marvel at the majestic Waimea Bay and the legendary Banzai Pipeline. Cap off your day with a visit to the Polynesian Cultural Center, where you can witness captivating performances celebrating the diverse cultures of the Pacific Islands.

Day Three: Island-Hopping to Maui
Bid farewell to Oahu as you set sail for the enchanting island of Maui, known for its pristine beaches, dramatic landscapes, and vibrant arts scene. Upon arrival, embark on a scenic drive along the legendary Road to Hana, a winding coastal highway that offers breathtaking views of lush rainforests, towering waterfalls, and rugged coastline. Stop at the quaint towns and hidden gems along the way, such as the charming village of Paia and the tranquil Waianapanapa State Park. As you reach Hana, immerse yourself in the serene beauty of its black sand beaches and tranquil pools, where you can take a refreshing dip in the crystal-clear waters. In the evening, treat yourself to a sumptuous feast of fresh seafood at one of Maui's renowned oceanfront

restaurants, where you can savor the flavors of the island while enjoying panoramic views of the sunset over the Pacific.

Day Four: Embracing Adventure on the Big Island

Venture into the heart of Hawaii Island, also known as the Big Island, where you'll discover a land of fiery volcanoes, lush rainforests, and cascading waterfalls. Begin your day with a visit to Hawaii Volcanoes National Park, home to the world's most active volcano, Kilauea. Explore the otherworldly landscapes of the park, where steam vents hiss and lava flows carve through the earth, leaving behind a stark and mesmerizing tableau. Afterward, journey to the summit of Mauna Kea, the tallest mountain in the world when measured from its base on the ocean floor. Here, you can witness the awe-inspiring spectacle of the night sky from the summit's renowned observatories, where astronomers peer into the depths of the universe. End your day with a relaxing soak in the natural hot springs of Ahalanui Park, where you can unwind amidst the tranquil beauty of the island's volcanic landscapes.

Day Five: Farewell to Paradise

As your time in Hawaii draws to a close, take one last opportunity to savor the island's beauty and tranquility. Spend your final morning exploring the picturesque beaches and charming towns of the Big Island, collecting memories to last a lifetime. Indulge in a leisurely brunch at a local cafe, where you can savor the flavors of Hawaii one last time before bidding farewell to paradise. As you board your flight home, carry with you the spirit of Aloha that permeates every corner of the islands, and treasure the memories of your unforgettable journey through the tropical paradise of Hawaii.

11.3 Safety Tips and Emergency Contacts

Hawaii, with its stunning beaches, lush landscapes, and vibrant culture, is a dream destination for many travelers. However, like any other place, it's essential to prioritize safety during your visit to ensure a memorable and incident-free experience. Whether you're exploring the volcanic wonders of Big Island or basking in the sun on Waikiki Beach, being prepared and informed about safety measures and emergency contacts is crucial.

Safety Tips

Water Safety

Hawaii's crystal-clear waters are inviting, but they can also pose risks, especially for those unfamiliar with ocean conditions. Always swim at lifeguarded beaches and heed warning signs about strong currents or jellyfish presence. If you're not a confident swimmer, consider wearing a life jacket. Additionally, be cautious of coral reefs, as they can cause injuries if you accidentally step on them.

Hiking Safety

Hawaii's diverse landscapes offer fantastic hiking opportunities, but it's essential to prepare adequately. Research your chosen trail beforehand, wear appropriate footwear, and bring plenty of water and snacks. Stay on marked paths, as venturing off-trail can be dangerous, especially near cliffs or steep terrain. If you're hiking in remote areas, inform someone of your plans and estimated return time.

Wildlife Awareness: Hawaii is home to unique flora and fauna, including endangered species like the Hawaiian monk seal and green sea turtle. While encountering wildlife can be thrilling, maintain a respectful distance and never attempt to touch or feed them. Some plants and animals in Hawaii are also poisonous, so familiarize yourself with potential hazards before exploring.

Driving Safety: If you're planning to rent a car to explore the islands, familiarize yourself with Hawaii's traffic laws and road conditions. Keep an eye out for wildlife crossing roads, especially in rural areas, and be mindful of narrow, winding roads common on islands like Maui and Kauai. Avoid distracted driving, and always wear your seatbelt.

Emergency Contacts

Emergency Services

In case of any emergency, dial 911 for immediate assistance. Whether it's a medical emergency, a natural disaster, or a criminal incident, trained professionals are available 24/7 to provide aid and support.

Hawaiian Islands Visitor Emergency Response Program (V.E.R.P.): V.E.R.P. is a statewide initiative aimed at assisting visitors during emergencies or crises. They offer a helpline (1-855-774-8277) that provides information and support in multiple languages. Additionally, V.E.R.P. collaborates with various agencies to ensure timely and effective responses to visitor-related incidents.

Local Hospitals and Medical Centers: Familiarize yourself with the locations of hospitals and medical centers in the area you're visiting. In case of a medical emergency, knowing where to go for prompt medical attention can make a significant difference. Keep important medical information and insurance details handy.

Coast Guard: For maritime emergencies or water-related incidents, contact the U.S. Coast Guard at their toll-free number, 1-800-323-7233. Whether it's a boating accident, a swimmer in distress, or a missing person at sea, the Coast Guard is equipped to handle various maritime emergencies.

11.4 Shopping and Souvenirs

SHOPPING IN HAWAII

Directions from Ala Moana Center, Ala Moana Boulevard, Honolulu, HI, USA to Kahala Mall, Waialae Avenue, Honolulu, HI, USA

A
Ala Moana Center, Ala Moana Boulevard, Honolulu, HI, USA

B
McCully Shopping Center, Kapiolani Boulevard, Honolulu, HI, USA

C
Kaimuki Shopping Center, Waialae Avenue, Honolulu, HI, USA

D
Royal Hawaiian Center, Kalākaua Avenue, Honolulu, HI, USA

E
Kapahulu Shopping Center, Kapahulu Avenue. Honolulu, HI USA

F
Waimalu Plaza Shopping Center ka ahumanu Street Aiea, HI, G

G
Hawai'i Kai Towne Center, Keahole Street, Honolulu, HI, USA

H
Kahala Mall, Waialae Avenue, Honolulu, HI, USA

Hawaii offers an array of shopping experiences for visitors seeking unique souvenirs and local treasures. From bustling shopping centers to quaint boutiques and antique stores, each location presents an opportunity to delve into the island's diverse offerings.

Hawaii Shopping Centre

Hawaii Shopping Centre stands as a haven for shoppers seeking both luxury and everyday essentials. Located conveniently in the heart of the city, this center boasts a plethora of boutiques, ranging from high-end fashion labels to locally crafted goods. Visitors can explore a variety of products, including traditional Hawaiian apparel, artisanal jewelry, and tropical home décor. Prices vary depending on the item and brand, with options suitable for every budget. The center typically opens at 10:00 AM and closes around 9:00 PM, providing ample time for leisurely browsing and shopping. Accessible via public transportation or by car, it offers a central location for indulging in retail therapy while exploring Honolulu's vibrant urban landscape.

Ala Moana Center

As one of the largest open-air shopping centers globally, Ala Moana Center stands as a premier destination for both locals and tourists alike. Situated near Waikiki Beach, this expansive complex features over 350 stores, ranging from internationally renowned brands to local artisans. Visitors can peruse a diverse selection of merchandise, including designer clothing, handmade crafts, and gourmet treats. Prices vary widely, catering to a broad spectrum of shoppers. With operating hours extending from morning till night, Ala Moana Center accommodates varying schedules and preferences. Conveniently accessible via public transit or private vehicle, it offers ample parking and shuttle services for added convenience.

McCully Shopping Center

Tucked away in the bustling neighborhood of McCully, McCully Shopping Center offers a quaint yet vibrant shopping experience. Boasting an eclectic mix of boutique stores and specialty shops, this hidden gem caters to discerning shoppers seeking unique finds. From vintage clothing and retro collectibles to local artwork and handmade souvenirs, the center's offerings reflect the rich tapestry of Hawaiian culture. Prices at McCully Shopping Center tend to be reasonable, making it an ideal destination for budget-conscious travelers. Opening hours vary by store, but most establishments welcome visitors from mid-morning until early evening. Accessible via public transportation or by foot, the center provides a convenient respite from the hustle and bustle of downtown Honolulu.

Kaimuki Shopping Center

Kaimuki Shopping Center offers a laid-back shopping experience infused with local charm. This intimate complex houses an eclectic mix of boutiques, galleries, and specialty stores, each offering its own unique selection of goods. Visitors can browse through an array of Hawaiian-inspired clothing, handmade jewelry, and artisanal crafts, all crafted with meticulous attention to detail. Prices at Kaimuki Shopping Center range from affordable to upscale, catering to a diverse clientele. Operating hours typically span from late morning to early evening, allowing ample time for leisurely exploration. Easily accessible by car or public transit, the center exudes a relaxed atmosphere that invites visitors to immerse themselves in the essence of island living.

Royal Hawaiian Center

Situated amidst the bustling streets of Waikiki, Royal Hawaiian Center stands as a beacon of luxury and sophistication. Home to an impressive array of designer boutiques, upscale retailers, and gourmet eateries, this iconic destination offers a shopping experience unlike any other. Visitors can peruse exclusive collections of high-end fashion, fine jewelry, and luxury goods, all set against the backdrop of Hawaii's vibrant cultural heritage. Prices at Royal Hawaiian Center reflect the prestige of its offerings, with options available for discerning shoppers with refined tastes. Operating hours extend into the evening, allowing visitors to indulge in after-hours shopping and dining. Easily accessible by foot or public transit, the center serves as a luxurious oasis amidst the bustling energy of Waikiki.

Kapahulu Shopping Center

Located just minutes from Waikiki Beach, Kapahulu Shopping Center offers a diverse array of shopping and dining options in a relaxed, neighborhood setting. Visitors can explore a mix of local boutiques, specialty stores, and ethnic eateries, each offering its own unique charm. From Hawaiian apparel and surf gear to handmade crafts and souvenirs, the center's offerings reflect the eclectic spirit of island life. Prices at Kapahulu Shopping Center tend to be moderate, making it an ideal destination for budget-conscious travelers seeking authentic Hawaiian treasures. Operating hours vary by store, but most establishments welcome visitors from mid-morning until early evening. Conveniently accessible by car or public transit, the center provides a convenient stop for those exploring the vibrant neighborhoods of Honolulu.

Wai'anae Mall

Located on the west coast of Oahu, Wai'anae Mall offers a unique shopping experience amidst the natural beauty of the Hawaiian countryside. This intimate complex features a mix of local vendors, specialty shops, and casual eateries, catering to the needs of residents and visitors alike. Visitors can browse through a variety of goods, including handmade crafts, locally sourced products, and island-inspired souvenirs. Prices at Wai'anae Mall are generally affordable, reflecting the laid-back atmosphere of the surrounding community. Operating hours vary by store, but most establishments are open from mid-morning until early evening. Accessible by car or public transit, the mall offers ample parking and a relaxed ambiance that invites visitors to unwind and explore at their own pace.

Waimalu Plaza Shopping Center

Conveniently located in Aiea, Waimalu Plaza Shopping Center offers a diverse array of shopping and dining options in a convenient, centralized location. This bustling complex features a mix of national retailers, local boutiques, and ethnic eateries, catering to the diverse tastes of its patrons. Visitors can peruse a variety of goods, including clothing, accessories, electronics, and household items, all set against the backdrop of Hawaii's stunning natural beauty. Prices at Waimalu Plaza Shopping Center vary depending on the retailer and product category, with options available for every budget. Operating hours extend into the evening, allowing visitors to shop and dine at their leisure. Easily accessible by car or public transit, the center provides ample parking and a vibrant atmosphere that captures the spirit of island living.

Hawai'i Kai Towne Center

Perched on the scenic shores of Maunalua Bay, Hawai'i Kai Towne Center offers a premier shopping and dining destination in East Honolulu. This waterfront complex features a mix of upscale retailers, local boutiques, and casual eateries, all set against the backdrop of Hawaii's breathtaking natural beauty. Visitors can explore a variety of goods, including designer clothing, artisanal crafts, and gourmet treats, all curated with the discerning shopper in mind. Prices at Hawai'i Kai Towne Center range from affordable to upscale, catering to a diverse clientele. Operating hours extend into the evening, allowing visitors to shop, dine, and soak in the sunset views. Easily accessible by car, the center offers ample parking and a relaxed ambiance that invites visitors to linger and explore.

Kahala Mall

Situated in the upscale neighborhood of Kahala, Kahala Mall offers a sophisticated shopping experience amidst the serene beauty of Hawaii's southeastern coastline. This premier shopping destination features a curated selection of upscale boutiques, luxury retailers, and gourmet eateries, catering to the discerning tastes of its patrons. Visitors can peruse a variety of goods, including designer clothing, fine jewelry, and artisanal home décor, all set against the backdrop of Kahala's lush landscapes. Prices at Kahala Mall reflect the prestige of its offerings, with options available for discerning shoppers seeking luxury and refinement. Operating hours extend into the evening, allowing visitors to shop, dine, and unwind in style. Easily accessible by car, the mall offers valet parking and a sophisticated ambiance that captures the essence of island luxury.

11.5 Useful Websites, Mobile Apps and Online Resources

Exploring Hawaii's stunning landscapes and vibrant culture requires careful planning and access to reliable resources. From finding the best local eats to discovering hidden gems off the beaten path, these five websites and mobile apps offer valuable tools and information to enhance your Hawaiian experience.

Hawaii Tourism Authority Website

The Hawaii Tourism Authority website serves as a comprehensive guide for visitors looking to explore the islands. Here, you can find information on accommodations, activities, events, and transportation options across all four main islands: Oahu, Maui, Big Island, and Kauai. The website features interactive maps, travel guides, and insider tips to help you plan your itinerary and make the most of your time in Hawaii.

GoHawaii Mobile App

The GoHawaii mobile app is the perfect companion for travelers on the go. Available for both iOS and Android devices, this app offers a wealth of information and features to enhance your Hawaiian adventure. From finding nearby attractions and activities to accessing exclusive deals and discounts, the GoHawaii app has everything you need to make the most of your trip. One of the standout features of the GoHawaii app is its offline map functionality, which allows you to navigate the islands even without an internet connection. You can download maps of Oahu, Maui, Big Island, and Kauai in advance, ensuring that you always have access to essential navigation tools wherever your travels take you.

Yelp

When it comes to finding the best local eats in Hawaii, Yelp is a must-have app for foodies. With millions of user-generated reviews and ratings, Yelp makes it easy to discover top-rated restaurants, cafes, food trucks, and more across the islands. Whether you're craving fresh seafood, traditional Hawaiian cuisine, or international fare, you can find it all on Yelp. In addition to restaurant recommendations, Yelp also provides information on nearby attractions, shopping destinations, and recreational activities. You can use the app to read reviews, view photos, and even make reservations directly from your smartphone, ensuring a seamless dining experience wherever you go in Hawaii.

AllTrails

For outdoor enthusiasts and nature lovers, AllTrails is a must-have app for exploring Hawaii's breathtaking landscapes. With thousands of trails to choose from, ranging from easy strolls to challenging hikes, AllTrails offers something for every skill level and interest. You can use the app to discover hidden waterfalls, scenic viewpoints, and pristine beaches off the beaten path. One of the standout features of AllTrails is its detailed trail maps, which provide information on trail length, elevation gain, difficulty level, and user reviews. You can also track your progress in real-time using GPS navigation, ensuring that you stay on course during your outdoor adventures in Hawaii.

Shaka Guide

Shaka Guide is a popular audio tour app that offers self-guided driving tours of Hawaii's most iconic attractions and scenic routes. With GPS navigation and offline maps, you can explore at your own pace while listening to engaging commentary from local experts. Shaka Guide offers a variety of tour options, including cultural tours, scenic drives, and historical walks, allowing you to customize your Hawaiian experience to suit your interests. One of the unique features of Shaka Guide is its ability to provide turn-by-turn directions and points of interest along the way, ensuring that you don't miss any hidden gems or photo opportunities. Whether you're cruising along the Road to Hana or exploring the volcanic landscapes of Big Island, Shaka Guide is your ultimate companion for discovering the beauty of Hawaii.

11.6 Internet Access and Connectivity

Staying connected while traveling is essential for many visitors. Whether it's sharing breathtaking photos of Hawaii's landscapes on social media or accessing important information online, having reliable internet access enhances the overall travel experience. Fortunately, Hawaii offers various options for internet connectivity to suit different preferences and needs.

Hotel and Resort Wi-Fi

Many hotels and resorts across Hawaii provide complimentary Wi-Fi access to their guests. This option is convenient for travelers who prefer to stay connected within the comfort of their accommodations. Before booking your stay, inquire about the availability and quality of Wi-Fi services to ensure a smooth online experience during your visit.

Mobile Data Plans

For visitors who prefer the flexibility of staying connected on the go, purchasing a local SIM card or activating an international roaming plan can be a convenient option. Several mobile network providers offer prepaid SIM cards with data packages tailored to tourists' needs. Additionally, international travelers can inquire with their home network providers about roaming options in Hawaii.

Portable Wi-Fi Hotspots

Another popular option for internet connectivity in Hawaii is renting a portable Wi-Fi hotspot. These pocket-sized devices allow multiple devices to connect to the internet simultaneously, making them ideal for families or groups traveling together. Portable Wi-Fi hotspot rental services are available at airports, tourist information centers, and online platforms, offering flexible rental durations to suit different travel itineraries.

Public Wi-Fi Hotspots

Hawaii's major cities and tourist hubs are equipped with public Wi-Fi hotspots, allowing visitors to stay connected while exploring popular attractions or dining at local restaurants. While convenient, it's essential to exercise caution when connecting to public Wi-Fi networks, as they may not always be secure. Avoid accessing sensitive information or making online transactions while connected to public Wi-Fi to prevent potential security risks.

Internet Cafés and Co-working Spaces

For travelers who require a dedicated workspace or reliable internet access for work or business purposes, internet cafés and co-working spaces are available in urban areas like Honolulu and Maui. These establishments offer high-speed internet connections, printing facilities, and other amenities designed to cater to the needs of digital nomads, freelancers, and business travelers.

11.7 Visitor Centers and Tourist Assistance

Amidst this paradise of natural beauty and cultural richness, navigating your way through the islands can be both exhilarating and overwhelming. That's where visitor centers and tourist assistance come into play, serving as beacons of guidance and resources to ensure that your Hawaiian adventure is nothing short of extraordinary. From Honolulu International Airport to the rugged terrain of the Big Island, these centers stand ready to welcome you with open arms and provide you with the tools and information you need to make the most of your time in paradise. So let's delve into the world of visitor centers and tourist assistance, as we embark on an unforgettable journey through the enchanting islands of Hawaii.

Honolulu International Airport
As the primary entry point for travelers to Hawaii, Honolulu International Airport serves as the first port of call for visitors seeking assistance and information. Here, travelers can find a wealth of resources to aid in their exploration of the islands, including information desks staffed by knowledgeable personnel who can provide guidance on transportation options, accommodation recommendations, and local attractions. Additionally, the airport features tourist assistance centers where visitors can obtain maps, brochures, and other helpful materials to enhance their Hawaiian experience.

Waikiki Visitor Center
Situated in the heart of Honolulu's bustling Waikiki district, the Waikiki Visitor Center serves as a hub for tourists seeking information and assistance during their stay. Here, visitors can access a wide range of services, including

personalized itinerary planning, activity bookings, and dining recommendations. The center's friendly and knowledgeable staff are on hand to provide expert guidance on everything from snorkeling excursions to cultural events, ensuring that visitors make the most of their time in paradise. Located at 2270 Kalakaua Avenue, the Waikiki Visitor Center is easily accessible and open daily to serve the needs of travelers.

Hawaii Volcanoes National Park Visitor Center

For travelers seeking to explore the dramatic landscapes and fascinating geological wonders of the Big Island, the Hawaii Volcanoes National Park Visitor Center is an essential resource. Located within the park itself, this visitor center offers a wealth of information on the park's history, geology, and wildlife, as well as helpful tips for exploring its vast expanse. Knowledgeable park rangers are on hand to provide guidance and assistance to visitors, helping them plan their adventures and navigate the park's trails and attractions safely. Additionally, the visitor center features exhibits, films, and interpretive programs that offer insight into the unique natural and cultural heritage of the area, making it an indispensable stop for anyone visiting the Big Island.

Haleakalā National Park Visitor Center

Perched on the rim of the majestic Haleakalā Crater on the island of Maui, the Haleakalā National Park Visitor Center offers visitors a gateway to the awe-inspiring landscapes and biodiversity of the park. Here, visitors can learn about the park's geological history, native flora and fauna, and cultural significance through interactive exhibits and interpretive programs. Park rangers are available to provide guidance and assistance to visitors, whether they're embarking on a hike through the crater, stargazing at the park's renowned observatory, or simply soaking in the breathtaking views of the surrounding landscape. Located at 7000 feet above sea level, the visitor center provides a unique opportunity to experience the natural beauty and tranquility of Maui's upcountry.

Polynesian Cultural Center

Immerse yourself in the rich cultural heritage of the Pacific Islands at the Polynesian Cultural Center, located on the northeastern shore of Oahu. As one of Hawaii's premier tourist attractions, the center offers visitors a chance to experience the traditions, music, dance, and cuisine of Polynesia through immersive exhibits, live performances, and interactive demonstrations. In addition to its cultural offerings, the Polynesian Cultural Center provides a range of visitor services, including dining options, souvenir shops, and guided tours, ensuring that guests have everything they need for an unforgettable cultural experience. Located at 55-370 Kamehameha Highway in Laie, the center is easily accessible from Honolulu and other major tourist destinations on Oahu.

CONCLUSION AND RECOMMENDATIONS

As you close the pages of this travel guide, you're not just shutting a book; you're opening the door to an unforgettable adventure in the breathtaking paradise that is Hawaii. From the moment you set foot on its sandy shores, you'll be greeted by warm ocean breezes, vibrant culture, and the spirit of aloha that permeates every corner of these islands. But before you embark on your journey, allow us to leave you with a few insider tips to ensure your experience is nothing short of magical.

Insider Tips/Recommendations:

Embrace the Aloha Spirit: The true essence of Hawaii lies not just in its stunning landscapes but also in the kindness and hospitality of its people. Take the time to connect with locals, learn about their traditions, and don't be afraid to say "aloha" with a smile.

Explore Beyond the Tourist Hotspots: While iconic attractions like Waikiki Beach and Pearl Harbor are must-sees, don't hesitate to venture off the beaten path. Explore hidden beaches, hike through lush rainforests, and discover charming local eateries to truly immerse yourself in the authentic Hawaiian experience.

Respect the Environment: Hawaii's natural beauty is unparalleled, and it's our responsibility as visitors to preserve and protect it. Practice responsible tourism by leaving no trace, supporting eco-friendly businesses, and following all guidelines for conservation and sustainability.

Dive into Hawaiian Cuisine: One of the best ways to experience a destination is through its food, and Hawaii is no exception. Indulge in fresh seafood, tropical fruits, and traditional dishes like poke and poi. Don't forget to try shave ice for a refreshing treat that's a local favorite.

Embrace Adventure: Whether you're a thrill-seeker or a nature lover, Hawaii offers endless opportunities for adventure. From surfing the legendary waves of the North Shore to snorkeling with colorful marine life, challenge yourself to step out of your comfort zone and create memories that will last a lifetime.

Hawaii is more than just a destination; it's a state of mind, a feeling of pure bliss that washes over you from the moment you arrive. Your Hawaiian adventure awaits, and trust us, it's worth every moment. Aloha and mahalo for choosing Hawaii – we can't wait to welcome you with open arms……

Made in the USA
Monee, IL
05 January 2025

76156897R00090